CW00408483

BECKHAMPTON
TIME PRESENT AND TIME PAST

TIME PRESENT AND TIME PAST
ARE BOTH PERHAPS PRESENT IN TIME FUTURE
AND TIME FUTURE CONTAINED IN TIME PAST

T.S. Eliot, Burnt Norton

Beckhampton

TIME PRESENT
AND
TIME PAST

Patricia Parslew

illustrated by Jane Brunning

First published in the United Kingdom in 2004 by
The Hobnob Press, PO Box 1838, East Knoyle, Salisbury SP3 6FA

© Patricia Parslew 2004 (text)
© Jane Brunning 2004 (illustrations)

All rights reserved. No part of this publication may be reproduced, stored in a retrieval system, or transmitted, in any form or by any means, electronic, mechanical, photo-copying, recording or otherwise, without the prior permission of the publisher and copyright holder.

British Library Cataloguing in Publication Data
A catalogue record for this book is available from the British Library.

ISBN 0-946418-28-4

Typeset in 11/15 pt Scala
Typesetting and origination by John Chandler
Printed in Great Britain by Salisbury Printing Company Ltd, Salisbury

Patricia Parslew *was for some time a special school teacher, then ran the bookshops in Bodmin, Cornwall, and Hungerford with her husband. She is now retired, and living in East Anglia.*

Jane Brunning *is an artist who lives in Beckhampton. She celebrates in her work the downland landscape and the lines of humans and animals that have interwoven with this special place over the last 5,000 or so years.*

Introduction

BECKHAMPTON IS, in the view of most of its inhabitants, special. This book attempts to explain why – as far as one can explain what amounts to an emotional reaction. Perhaps part of that reaction is the knowledge that people have lived and worked here for thousands of years.

When I became one of the team working on our Millennium book in 1999 I began to appreciate that the village, although on the surface an insignificant dwelling-place, possessed a wealth of history, both its own, and that of the surrounding area. From the Stone Age to the twenty-first century the residents of Beckhampton have been onlookers or partakers of many events, great and small. There is a feeling of timelessness here, where modern people co-exist with prehistoric remains. By presenting the facts I hope to build up a picture of the village, and perhaps bring an insight to its character.

Because records pertaining directly to the village are relatively few, I have included events which occurred within a few miles' radius, which have had some influence on Beckhampton and its residents.

In many ways, this is a history of any North Wiltshire village, yet time and again Beckhampton has proved to be different. Apart from fact and feeling, there is still something about the present village that is impossible to pin down. We who live here are privileged: in an indefinable way.

Beckhampton is, I repeat, special.

Acknowledgements

M Y THANKS are due to:

Dr. John Chandler, Historian, Publisher, Editor, for all his help, advice and encouragement.

Dr. Lorna Haycock, Sandell Library, Wiltshire Heritage Museum, Devizes, for help with many hours of research.

Dr. Paul Robinson, Curator, Wiltshire Heritage Museum, Devizes, for showing me, and allowing Jane to draw, many artefacts not on display.

Roger Charlton, Beckhampton House Stables, for the loan of his book, and much help with the recent history of the stables.

Avebury Parish Council, for a bursary.

The villagers themselves, especially the Hues family.

My husband, Michael, for his constant encouragement and enthusiasm.

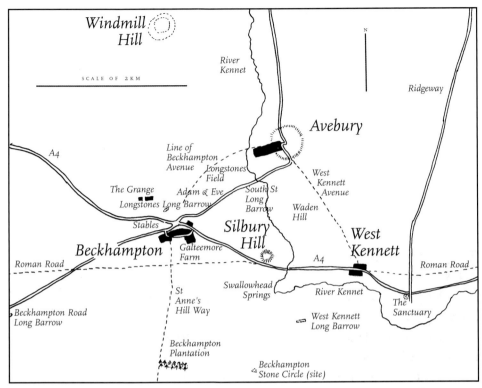

Beckhampton and its immediate surroundings (above); and further afield (below)

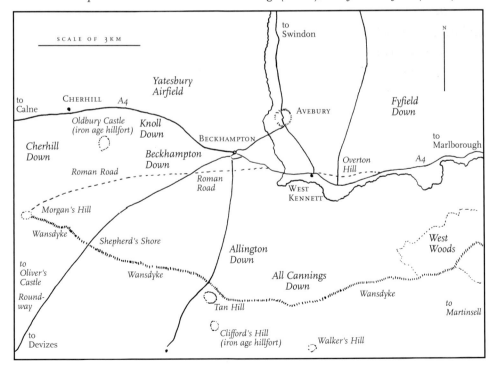

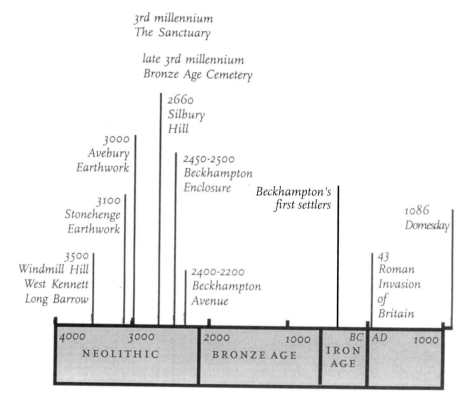

3rd millennium
The Sanctuary

late 3rd millennium
Bronze Age Cemetery

2660
Silbury
Hill

3000
Avebury
Earthwork

2450-2500
Beckhampton
Enclosure

Beckhampton's
first settlers

3100
Stonehenge
Earthwork

1086
Domesday

3500
Windmill Hill
West Kennett
Long Barrow

2400-2200
Beckhampton
Avenue

43
Roman
Invasion
of
Britain

| 4000 | 3000 | 2000 | 1000 | BC | AD | 1000 |
| NEOLITHIC | | BRONZE AGE | | IRON AGE | | |

A Beckhampton timechart

B ECKHAMPTON IS A HIDDEN VILLAGE.
It is there, on the map and signposts, yet it is relatively unknown to anyone outside the immediate area. It has always lain in the shadow of its more illustrious neighbour, Avebury, within whose parish it lies. Those travelling along the A4 today will identify the crossroads, the pub, the racing stables – perhaps the farm. Few realise that there is also a community of some 45 houses and 150 people. The village is, largely, content to remain hidden.

Today's settlement gives little clue to the changes which the village has undergone through the centuries. Most of the houses are modern; most spread along the lane (which has no name) connecting the Marlborough and Devizes roads. The present population is shifting: during the past ten years a good third of the houses have changed hands. But the spirit of community has remained; it is a friendly place, its residents, if they are not on first-name terms, greeting each other with a cheery wave. The social events of the twenty-first century involving the whole village have been well-attended and enjoyable.

The village is set in one of the many shallow valleys of the Marlborough Downs, and is surrounded by trees which almost completely shield the houses. At the eastern end lies the farm, with its Georgian house set back from a broad lawn. Horses and cattle graze in adjoining fields; the former, appearing in the lane on a daily basis, adding to the timeless feeling of the place. At the western end are the racing stables, with another beautiful Georgian house overlooking the crossroads. Today they are bustling; their employees accounting for a good proportion of the population. One of the unforgettable sights of Beckhampton is a string of race horses setting off for their early morning exercise on the gallops on Beckhampton Down: if the morning is frosty and slightly misty the scene is breathtaking.

Three market towns have served the village in one way or another through the centuries. Marlborough, Devizes and Calne are all more or less seven miles away, so the villagers have had some choice for shopping and trading.

North of the village are extensive views across the old airfield of Yatesbury round to the present Ridgeway. Avebury is nestling below the hills, also hidden within trees, the fifteenth century church tower revealing its presence. Windmill Hill is not immediately obvious, in spite of its importance. When one is standing there amongst the ancient earthworks its dominance is striking; in the larger context of the surrounding downs the hill blends into the landscape.

Half a mile east of the village and at one time very much part of the local farms lies Silbury Hill, the largest man-made mound in Europe. It is often surrounded by a 'moat' during the winter months as the ditches formed when the hill was dug fill with water. It has suffered many indignities over the years: invasion by excavation, crowds celebrating a fair on Palm Sunday, with children (and maybe adults) sliding down its steep sides, more lately an ugly fence protecting a large, temporarily filled, cavity on the top. In spite of this, it is difficult to take the hill for granted, even when viewed every day: although our knowledge of it has grown during the last few years, it is still an object of mystery and splendour.

East of Silbury hill the young river Kennet flows – except in dry weather. Just south of the hill it turns sharp left at Swallowhead Springs. For many years – and indeed to this day – the springs were thought to be the source of the Kennet. This may well be true, since that part of the river above the springs was known as the 'Winterbourne' i.e. a river or stream which flows only during the winter in wet conditions. A recently-published map of the river names the source as Uffcott – and so the controversy continues. These days the springs are often dry, even in winter, with the river only gathering pace further down the valley.

South of the village the downs rise gently. This land, formerly pasture, is all cultivated today, different crops ensuring a changing outlook through the seasons. Here are the skylarks, the hares, and perhaps a deer or two. The twenty-first century still intrudes in the shape of air traffic: helicopters and hang gliders, motorised or wind-powered; airliners above them all. But among the downs there is a real feeling of moving back in time: the shape of the hills does not change; it takes little imagination to see them as they were four thousand years ago. After levelling out, the ground again rises until it reaches the Tan Hill escarpment overlooking Pewsey Vale. This is the southernmost point of the Marlborough Downs. Here, at nearly 1,000 feet above sea level the views are stunning; the turf which has been grazed for centuries rich in wild flowers.

Butler's Cottage, Beckhampton, from the byway

There are many ancient trackways on these downs; the best known, and perhaps the oldest, the Ridgeway. One such track runs from Avebury, past Silbury Hill and on due South to Beckhampton Penning. Another leads due south from the western end of the village. It was known as 'St.Anne's Hill Way' in the eighteenth century; some years ago the signpost pointed to 'All Cannings'; now it is merely a 'Byway'. This path crosses the Roman road, at this point only discernible by tracing its length from Morgan's Hill in the distance. There are many Saxon roads or 'herepaths' in the area, one of which passes through Beckhampton. Another is preserved today as the Wessex Ridgeway for some of its length.

Mid way between the village and the Tan Hill escarpment is Beckhampton plantation – a line of trees well over a century old. Nobody knows why it was planted (or exactly when) but it is an unmistakable feature of the landscape. And everywhere the barrows, now the only visible indication of the prehistory of the immediate area, since their very shape has defeated the plough.

Beckhampton is not unique in its ancient origins, certainly not in this part of North Wiltshire, where most towns and villages existed well before Domesday. But in the context of the country as a whole, it is, perhaps, unusual for a village to be able to trace its history back to the Bronze Age; and to be able to state that occupancy has been continuous for more than four thousand years. Not quite a proven statement, but a very reasonable assumption.

The story begins around 5,500 years ago, when Neolithic people settled on Windmill Hill, about one and a half miles north of Beckhampton. These early settlers established a lasting and notable site. The many remains, including pottery, animal and human bones point to an important centre: a gathering place, possibly for tribes outside the area, to exchange news and trade, and indulge in feasting and other ceremonies of the living and the dead.

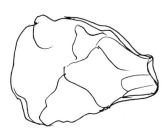

Their life-style was comparatively sophisticated. Pottery was used, some of it decorated, some made of non-local clay. Cups and bowls, storage jars and large, open vessels for cooking have been found on the site. Flint and animal bone provided tools – scrapers, knives, arrowheads, axes, and, not the least important, cattle scapulas for digging. Evidence has been found of the use of a simple wooden plough: the earliest recorded use of such an implement in Europe. Although these people cultivated the land, their main diet was cattle and other meat, indicated by the preponderance of these bones in the ditches around Windmill Hill.

Neolithic polished flint axe

They created many long barrows, some of which were used for burial, others, perhaps, to mark boundaries, since evidence of burials has not been found in all of them. Three long barrows lie close to the present village of Beckhampton. The barrow easily

Neolithic discoidal scraper

visible from the crossroads, Longstones, was built as a series of bays, but the only evidence of burial was a late Bronze age urn with burnt bones; nothing was buried when the barrow was built. South Street barrow, just off the road leading to Avebury Trusloe, is not visible today, but again the only finds were pottery of a much later date than the barrow itself, although nine sarsens were discovered where burial might have taken place. These could have formed an earlier shrine. Beckhampton road barrow, south of the present Devizes road, has a similar history: no primary burial, but this time the barrow was constructed over a naturally occurring sarsen. (Sarsen is the local stone; a sand stone, it occurs as huge stones which form the basis of the many ancient monuments in the area. Stones on the surface are weathered into fantastic shapes which, with a little imagination, can be transformed into animals, trolls, even household objects.)

There was, possibly, another long barrow on the site of the present plantation: archaeological evidence is unsure on this point, and any evidence on

West Kennett long barrow

the ground has long since been ploughed out. But there can be no doubt about the most famous barrow in the area, that of West Kennett. This was a chambered tomb, the eastern end of which has been excavated to demonstrate the structure of the entire tomb, which would have been 100 metres long. Although about two miles from Windmill Hill, the barrow remained in use for some two hundred years, before it was finally sealed by the mighty megaliths which stand there today.

All these structures which have been excavated over the years are direct evidence of the way of life of the Windmill Hill settlers. Other aspects are more open to supposition. It is known that the Neolithic people were responsible for a number of small stone circles and enclosures whose purpose may only be surmised.

Beckhampton's own stone circle is marked on OS maps of the 1930s. It was due south of Silbury Hill, due east of the plantation. It was first noted by William Stukeley, an eighteenth century archaeologist, who spent much time recording the antiquities of North Wiltshire, later to be published in his book 'Abury, A Temple of the British Druids'. Stukeley described the circle as a long barrow 22 paces long....set round with stones taken away by Farmer Green, standing a dozen years ago one great stone at the head of it i.e. towards Overton Hill.

As far as we know, the circle was never excavated. Stukeley suggests that the shape was more of an oval, and the term 'barrow' does indicate a burial, but this can never be verified. In the 1920s, a 'slight mound' was noted, with many of the stones still visible on the surface. By 1950 these were lying in heaps, hardly any *in situ*. Today there is no sign of it at all.

View from the site of the Beckhampton stone circle. Silbury Hill to the left, Waden Hill to the right, with Swallowhead Springs in the middle distance

Beckhampton also has its own enclosure, which was discovered and excavated in 1999 and 2000 by a combined universities group exploring the stone avenue. This enclosure pre-dates and is set partly under the avenue. It has several causewayed entrances, and is smaller than other enclosures in the area. Its purpose remains a mystery. In 2003 another unexplained feature was discovered by the universities group inside the enclosure. This consisted of two gullies which met near the socket of one of the avenue's stones. It may be related to the Neolithic square enclosure on Windmill Hill. Archaeology can reveal these structures, but it cannot fully explain them.

It was as the fourth millennium BC drew to a close, (i.e. c3,000 BC) that our ancestors turned to more important projects. Twenty odd miles away, the first ditches at Stonehenge were dug. A little later, the Avebury circle was begun. Both monuments started as a circular earthwork: it would be several hundred years before stones were erected. During these centuries, the area would have been comparatively heavily populated, with many men required for the heavy work of digging huge ditches, and later hauling stones to their destinations, to say nothing of the hunters needed to feed them. Yet exactly how, or where they lived remains a matter of conjecture. There is evidence of settlements, mostly in the form of round houses. Their life style would have been similar to that of Windmill Hill. Chieftains and leaders were buried in barrows, often following cremation. Ordinary people must have been disposed of somewhere, but again the where and the how remain a mystery.

Bronze socketed spearhead, Middle Bronze Age, from Beckhampton Down

We have now reached the early Bronze Age. Pottery is becoming more decorative, and bronze is replacing flint for hunting and other tools. A lovely socketed spear-head was found on Beckhampton Down – the land to the west of the racing stables. The sockets were added so that the spear-head could be tied to the shaft and thus withdrawn complete, ready to use again. There are many examples in Devizes Museum.

If Bronze Age people left little record of their living, there are plenty of monuments to their dead. Barrows, both long and circular, abound in the area. There was a Bronze Age cemetery, north east of the crossroads, where thirteen barrows have been identified; there may have been more. Many of the barrows were opened and plundered in the years before archaeological evidence was recorded. Where finds have been preserved they have not been spectacular. Many cinerary urns with burnt bones have been found, also small grave goods such as bone or bronze pins, suggesting that the body was wearing a cloak. Flint arrowheads and flakes are often present, although the significance of the latter is not clear.

Several beakers have been found associated with burials near to sarsens. In 1911 the large stone in Longstones field known as 'Adam' fell; it was decided

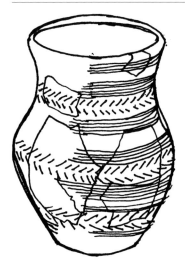

Longstones Beaker

to raise him the following year. While the hole in which the stone had stood was being cleared of rubble, remains of a human skeleton and fragments of a 'drinking cup or beaker' were discovered. It seems that the body had been buried beside the stone. The beaker was reconstructed and is now in Devizes Museum. 'Adam' was sunk in concrete and is now secure, although several feet lower in the ground than he would have been originally. Another beaker was found in a less well defined site beside the Devizes road. This time a sarsen was exposed in a ditch dug to lay water pipes in 1925. At its side were the remains of the beaker and some broken human bones. These finds are remarkable examples of Bronze Age skill, but the burials are relatively commonplace; nothing to rival the recent discovery at Amesbury of a Bronze Age warrior with over a hundred grave goods.

One burial, however, does stand out. It was not in a barrow, although near one, west of the Grange. It was discovered in March, 1948, when the down was ploughed for the first time. The ploughshares were damaged by a large, flat sarsen stone buried just beneath the surface. The farm hands disposed of the sarsen, and we can be thankful that the farm bailiff noticed that the ground beneath the stone had been disturbed. The site was excavated, and a circular grave was disclosed, containing the skeleton of a child of about five years of age. Also in the grave was a beaker with unusual decorations; a piece of chalk on which grooves had been cut, and two small flint flakes. It was impossible to determine the sex of the child, or to explain the artefacts found with it. As we have seen, beakers and flints were quite often interred with the body; the chalk implement may have been a toy. The remains were placed in the Alexander Keiller Museum at Avebury. The skeleton was recently sent away for restoration and preservation; it now lies in a humidity-controlled case, without its grave goods. It is a moving sight; one wonders whether his or her remains deserve more privacy. Yet its incredible poignancy arouses much sympathy with the modern visitor, and not a little perplexity. We shall never know who this Bronze Age child was, but we can offer our wonder, and respect.

For well over a millennium building continued on the major monuments. Stones were transported from Fyfield Down, (using methods which modern-day man has sought to emulate, without too much success) some to Stonehenge, some to Avebury, where the main circle and two inner ones were set up. It is easy to forget that at the time of building the ditches and enormous banks would have been white: an awe-inspiring sight at the time. One can but imagine the tremendous activity as the two monuments gradually took shape: the digging of trenches, cutting, dressing and final erection of the stones, with all the necessary earth slopes, log rolling and rope-making that would be entailed. Hunters would have been stretched to their limits, especially during the winter months, when life must have been exceedingly harsh.

As if two major monuments were not enough, 4,500 years ago work started on Silbury Hill – the most enigmatic of the three. In the eighteenth century it was thought to be a burial mound: legends grew about the fabulous statue of King Sil or Zel, mounted on his golden horse, himself clad in gold. Early etchings of the hill nearly always exaggerate its shape, making the slopes far steeper than their true angle of about 30 degrees. The hill is deceptively large. The stone circle of Stonehenge would fit upon its summit: human beings, viewed from below, are always much smaller than one would expect. There have been three major excavations of the hill (of which more anon) none of them throwing any light on the reason for its existence. Silbury will not give up its secrets yet.

The building at Avebury did not cease when the circles were completed. Two stone avenues were built roughly to the east and west, leading Stukeley to refer to them rather romantically as the Serpent's Head and Tail. That to the east, (the Head) now known as the West Kennet avenue, led to the Sanctuary – a timber and stone henge now set beside the A4, and marking the start of the Ridgeway. There is no doubt about the avenue's existence and direction, since many of its stones are still *in situ*.

The existence of the western, or Beckhampton avenue was questioned for many years, since apparently none of the stones remained. The two standing stones in Longstones field were thought to be unrelated to the monument. Recent excavation, however, has established that Beckhampton avenue did indeed exist; the two stones (known as Adam and Eve) being the sole remainders. 'Eve' is part of the avenue itself, 'Adam' forms one side of a cove – i.e. three huge stones placed as three sides of a square. The purpose of the cove – indeed the purpose of the avenues, is unclear. It is possible, due to the lack of archaeological finds within them, that the avenues were entered only by priests; the coves being places where common people could assemble, and be addressed.

We have seen that the Bronze Age was a time of intense activity in the area, yet we know little of the way of life of its people – more about the way of death. Towards the end of the era, Bronze Age Man, satisfied with the monuments which he had created (and unmindful of the puzzles they would present several millennia later) turned to more prosaic needs. Field systems began to be established; crops grown in the tilled earth. An agrarian system, instigated on Windmill Hill, evolved, which would exist, and be the main provider, until the twentieth century. The most significant change was the discovery of iron, and the ability to smelt it. Thus we move on to Beckhampton's first recorded residents.

At the end of the nineteenth century one Henry Cunnington excavated what he thought were 'pit dwellings' on Allington Down, near the brow of the long hill to the south of the present-day village. He reported on the two circular pits, inferring that they would be 'protected from the inclemencies of the weather by boughs of trees or sods of turf'. He found evidence of weaving in loom weights, and broken cooking pots. Signs of a fire reinforced his opinion that these were dwellings. The shepherd at the time informed him that there were many such pits 'on Mr. Wentworth's down'. In later years these 'dwellings' have been recognised as refuse pits, which in themselves indicate a settlement of some substance. This was probably a farmstead consisting of thatched wooden roundhouses, with enclosures or pounds for livestock – and several pits for refuse. (The latter a forerunner of our modern landfill sites.)

By now many varieties of grain were grown, and horses, similar to Exmoor ponies, had made an appearance. Cattle, sheep and goats continued to be herded. Tribes were becoming more nomadic, and trading developed: iron for tools and weapons, salt from the coast, and 'luxury' items such as jewellery. Coinage was introduced before the first century BC. It was thought that some of the tribes were becoming increasingly warlike, leading to the construction of the many hill forts in the region. Current thinking, however, indicates that not all of these hill forts were defensive. Some of the bigger ones, Martinsell for example, might have been built simply to enclose a settlement: to reinforce a sense of community.

Day to day life had changed little for hundreds of years. Our Iron Age settlers, not living within a fort, presumably led comparatively peaceful lives, tending their sheep and tilling their fields. We have no means of knowing whether they regarded Stonehenge, Avebury and Silbury as places of worship: they may not even have been aware of Stonehenge, but would certainly have known about Avebury and Silbury Hill. We do not know how long the Iron Age way of life would have continued, for there was a great upheaval on its way – the coming of the Romans.

T HE ROMANS did not so much invade Wiltshire as move in as of right. Battles had occurred at some of the Dorset hill forts, and there was some resistance within the county at first, but in all likelihood word had spread that they were here to stay, and defence would be a waste of time. Perhaps word also spread that these newcomers might prove advantageous.

The first change in the landscape was the building of the road. Its position is clearly visible today from Morgan's Hill, past Cherhill, then in a straight line to Silbury Hill. It is now mostly a rough track, muddy in winter, walkable in summer, although with some difficulty, owing to the deep ruts. Much of its length has been ploughed out.

To our Iron Age settlers, watching the building of the road just below their settlement, it must have been comparable to having a dual carriageway built through one's garden today. Then as now, opposition was useless – Progress must be accepted. As there were Roman artefacts amongst the Iron Age remains, we must assume that acceptance and some trading took place. In the

Roman road looking east to Silbury Hill and the site of the Roman town and Waden Hill

country as a whole Iron Age people gradually merged with the Roman way of life, and probably our Beckhampton settlers benefitted from the proximity of the road. There would have been a fair amount of traffic, as the road linked *Calleva* (Silchester) with *Aquae Sulis* (Bath). At the nearby town of *Cunetio* (near Marlborough) another road led to *Corinium* (Cirencester) – the most important town in western Britain: an administrative centre and the source of a particular style of mosaics.

There was a settlement on Waden Hill, facing Silbury Hill. Comparatively recent excavation has suggested that this was quite large, enough to merit the title 'small town'. Although Roman finds had been recorded there since the nineteenth century, the first intimation of a sizeable settlement came in 1993 when a pipeline was being dug. Substantial Roman structures were detected. An aerial survey in 1997 backed up the supposition that the remains were extensive. Present evidence suggests that the settlement covered 54 acres, on a North-South axis beside the Kennet, and an East-West axis alongside what is now the A4. There has been no excavation on the latter, and lack of crop marks have made it difficult to establish its extent. On the former, at least nine stone structures are now known. The first building was possibly of the second century; building continued into the fourth and fifth centuries.

Standing midway between *Verlucio* (Sandy Lane) and *Cunetio*, this town could have been a local administrative centre; plant remains suggest that some agriculture was carried out. Or, situated next to Silbury Hill, some sort of ritual or religious significance may have led to its rise. Most puzzling to archaeologists, four 'wells' have been discovered at the base of Silbury. One had been deliberately backfilled and sealed with huge sarsens. Within the well a column capital was found – it has not been removed, since this would necessitate a small crane at least. But its presence denotes either a large house or a temple. Was there a ring of these wells round the whole base of the hill? Were they, indeed, wells, or shafts with some other, perhaps ritual meaning? It may be that other such shafts will be found in the future. For now, our knowledge is only partial, but there is a wealth of remains waiting to be discovered by future archaeologists.

We know that there were several villas in the Beckhampton area. There was one at Cherhill, where the lovely hunting dog mosaic now in Devizes Museum was discovered. Another, south-west of Windmill Hill, also yielded a mosaic of a chequered design. Unfortunately this was not preserved, and traces of the villa have been destroyed. Roman villas were essentially farms, providing livelihood and shelter for those who worked there. The richer landowners would have had fine houses built, hence the mosaics. They would have access to such luxury items as silver, wine and jewellery. They continued the agricultural policies which they found; sheep and cattle herded, pigs and goats kept. Crops – oats, wheat, barley – were grown; enhanced by the 'new' pulses which the Romans introduced. In the fourth century AD a heavy taxation on grain was imposed, leading to more sheep-rearing. In Beckhampton, set amidst the downs, this would remain the staple form of agriculture until the twentieth century.

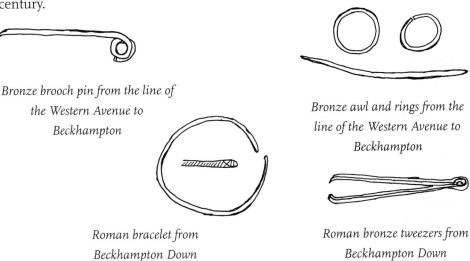

Bronze brooch pin from the line of
the Western Avenue to
Beckhampton

Bronze awl and rings from the
line of the Western Avenue to
Beckhampton

Roman bracelet from
Beckhampton Down

Roman bronze tweezers from
Beckhampton Down

There have been many notable Roman finds in the area, including domestic articles such as tweezers, tools, bracelets and brooches; perhaps the most unusual object being a pen knife in the shape of a leg. An important burial took place south of Beckhampton towards Tan Hill. A skeleton was found, lying full length, with a Roman vase at his head. Iron nails marked the shape of his coffin. Near Avebury Trusloe the burial of a child wearing jewellery was discovered.

Many Roman coins have been found; some in large quantities, suggesting deliberate burial – possibly towards the end of the Roman occupation. Doubtless not all the finds were recorded. One nineteenth century labourer is reported to have found a hoard; he is quoted as saying, 'When I were digging them big stones at Beckhampton I dug up lots on 'em [Roman coins] but I thought na one took no notice on 'em so I let 'em bide.' What a contrast to today's 'treasure hunters' with their metal detectors.

Which of our Roman forebears lost his key? Found at Beckhampton, this splendid object now rests in Devizes Museum, along with others of its kind.

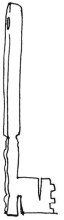

Some four to five inches long, the main shaft curves into a 'u' shape, finishing with teeth. Was it used for a storehouse, or did it open a more important door? Was there a duplicate, or did the door have to broken down? It is comforting to know that our ancestors were as careless with possessions as we are today.

These finds indicate a strong and busy Roman presence in the area, and the pattern of life was set – or so it seemed. But the Romans were not all-powerful: the empire shrank, and they withdrew from Britain. Once more Beckhampton faced a change, this time for the worse.

Roman iron
tumbler key
from Cherhill

Life under the Romans must have settled into an orderly and comparatively peaceful existence. When they left, during the fifth century AD, doubtless life carried on much as before for a while. But with no guiding overlords, systems broke down, trading became sporadic; the 'Dark Ages' had begun. Yet they were dark only in the sense that we know so little about them. The Anglo-Saxons produced some breathtakingly beautiful artefacts – the Sutton Hoo burial comes to mind. The simple churches which remain bear witness to clever use of building materials, and some lovely carving.

The first Saxons – the term has to be used to indicate invaders from the continent, particularly the low countries – arrived as raiders rather than settlers, although it is reasonable to suppose that as they moved further inland, their motives became domestic. They would have adapted settlements to their own use; any residents would have had to conform to their rule. Doubtless there were many conflicting loyalties at first, and indeed the next few centuries would prove to be unsettled, as tribes built up followers, and sought to overcome their enemies.

Nearer to home three graves, two of obviously important people, have been discovered. The Anglo-Saxons sometimes used Bronze Age barrows for their notable burials; (there were intrusive burials, thought to be fifth or sixth century, in the barrows on Overton Hill.) In the first case Silbury Hill was used. Stukeley reports that in 1723 Mr.Holford ordered some trees to be planted in the middle of the area at the top of the hill. We do not know if this order was ever carried out: but if it was, the trees would have been uprooted fifty years later when the first exploratory shaft into Silbury was sunk. As workmen were digging the ground ready for planting, they discovered the grave of a 'great king'. The bones were rotten, and perhaps Stukeley exaggerated a little in his description, for there were few grave goods: deer horns, an iron knife with a bone handle, two brass bits of money, and an item 'covered with rust' which turned out, after cleansing by Stukeley, to be an ornate horse's bit. Later research indicates that these items were not necessarily connected with the body, or possibly not found in the grave. But the burial, if not that of a king, must have been of a person of some importance.

One of the many round barrows surrounding Beckhampton. This one is just north of the Roman road

Not far away, on Roundway Down near Devizes, a seventh century burial was found, this time a woman. She was wearing jewellery: a necklace of gold pendants set with garnets and lignite, with gold wire beads. In her cloak were two pins linked by a chain, made of delicately worked gold, garnet and glass. These items can be seen in Devizes Museum – remnants of an age that was anything but dark. Devizes did not exist in Saxon times; the woman may have come from Potterne which was a sizeable settlement, with a pre-conquest church and baptistery.

The third burial was discovered in 2000 when 'Adam' (one of the stones in Longstones field) was being excavated. In this case no body was found, but the many iron fragments: including a spearhead, a shield fitting and part of a knife blade, indicate a Saxon burial, probably pagan.

It was the Saxon age that first brought Beckhampton into the range of national events – although at this stage the whole country was not involved. Set in a sort of 'no man's land' between the mighty kingdoms of Wessex and Mercia, it was not an altogether comfortable place to live. Two major battles were fought on Wansdyke, two miles away; and indeed may have been the reason for the building of the dyke. Both battles took place on or around what is now Walker's Hill on the Tan Hill escarpment. In 592AD the battle of *Wodnesbeorg* (Woden's Barrow, the long barrow on top of the hill now known as Adam's Grave) took place. The Anglo-Saxon Chronicle records that 'Ceawlin was expelled after great slaughter.' Did the people at Beckhampton hear the sounds of battle, or perhaps see some of the soldiers?

Were they co-opted to help in the building of the huge earthwork which was being built so near their dwellings? Such an undertaking must have required hundreds of men – and perhaps women, too – and must have been of vital importance at the time. The exact dating of Wansdyke has proved impossible, and there are many conflicting theories. Definitely post-Roman, it was known to exist by 892AD. The most likely time for its construction is

Looking west along the Wansdyke

thought to be the late sixth century: this supposition is based on the first great battle of the Wessex-Mercia conflict. But as the rivalry between the two tribes continued, it is equally possible that it was built much later. Peter Fowler, writing about the West Woods section of the dyke, puts forward the theory that it was built in the late fifth century. He suggests that its construction was based on Roman military thinking, against a possible invasion from Saxons in the Thames valley.

Whatever its date, it is impressive today, showing up as a scar on the smooth surface of the downs. Originally built in two sections, that to the west makes its way from the Mendips to just south of Bath. East Wansdyke is rather better preserved: it makes its unmistakable way across the downs, providing pleasant walking or riding for several miles. Starting from Morgan's Hill it travels east along the Tan Hill escarpment, and beyond. In the bluebells of West Woods, it loses its sense of direction, turning sharp right. Perhaps there was a camp or fort here? Or perhaps, as Peter Fowler thinks, it was maintaining the contour line. Beyond the woods, it turns left back to its original line, and is finally lost, just to the east of Savernake Forest. Today a path runs along its length, giving great pleasure to walkers and horse riders.

During the seventh and early eighth centuries the area was probably under Mercian rule. After the second great battle near Wansdyke, in 715AD, Beckhampton became part of the West Saxon kingdom of Ine. He died in 726AD, and was buried in Sherborne Abbey. The unrest continued. By the late ninth century Egbert had conquered Mercia and assumed overlordship of the southern English. But another foe was now threatening – the Danes were invading. Internal struggles had to be subsumed to the greater danger. Alfred appeared on the scene, and fought several battles in the area, finally defeating the Danes at Edington. Wessex was won, but the Danes remained. The nearest Alfred got to Beckhampton was when he met his brother at Swanborough Tump near Woodborough in Pewsey Vale. Each swore to care for the other's children should either of them die in the forthcoming battle.

With the coming of Alfred and the unity of the southern kingdoms, life settled down a little, and some sort of governmental order was imposed. Throughout all the preceding unrest we have no proof that the village continued to exist. But we have no proof that it did not, and there is circumstantial evidence that the settlement remained. The Iron Age community stayed on into Roman times, supported by agriculture; 'ham' and 'tun' are words of Saxon origin; a Saxon road ran through the likeliest site of the village. Thus the main staples of existence: food, water, shelter and communication were met.

Three Saxon finds were made in Beckhampton: a small fragment of a buckle depicting a man on horseback; and two brooches; one a lovely bronze buckle of simple design, the other a silver disc depicting the stylised animals forming a central cross, their claws towards the perimeter. All these objects would have belonged to persons of high status. By Domesday there was a sizeable settlement. It is therefore reasonable to assume that the village lived on, possibly under a thane, following the pattern of landowner and peasant which was becoming established.

Anglo-Saxon applied disc brooch with silver repoussé plate, 3.6 cms diameter

Armies need food, and the peasants would continue to herd sheep, and grow crops in the open field system which was also becoming established at this time. Some of them, ceorls or commoners, might own small strips of land. But sheep remained the most important livestock, and sheep, until the twentieth century, was what Beckhampton did best. In a way, there was no choice: the

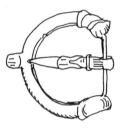

Late Saxon buckle

landscape decreed Man's use of it. The thin chalkland soils did not lend themselves to arable farming, therefore sheep, which could graze on the downs during the day, and be folded in fields at night, thereby fertilising the soil, were the most practical solution. Cattle, pigs and goats were also raised. Barley and wheat were the most important grains, for brewing and bread-making. Oats were grown, flax for cloth-making, woad for dyeing. Beans and peas brought in by the Romans continued to be grown. Houses were wooden, or lath and plaster – not very much different from the round houses of the Iron Age.

About a mile away, Avebury, which may have remained as a meeting place and place of worship for Iron Age and later tribes, had become a small Saxon town of some significance, occupying an area as big as the present village. Christianity had reached the area, for Avebury had its church. The present building contains remnants of the Saxon era. Beckhampton may have had a chapel: not recorded until the end of the twelfth century, we have no way of knowing when it was built.

The end of the first millennium AD, under Alfred's rule, saw a unification of the country, and a more peaceful regime. Although the year 976 was a year of great famine; with battles and dyke-building over, life in the village was set on an even keel. Shires and hundreds were established – the first recorded use of 'Wiltshire' was in the late ninth century. Each shire had its own earldorman or sheriff, (derived from 'shire-reeve') an early magistrate who was responsible for upholding the law. Cnut kept the West Saxon shires in his own hands, then in 1018 Godwin became Earl of Wessex – a huge earldom.

Market and trading towns sprang up; the two nearest being Calne and Marlborough, which had its own mint. There were also mints at Wilton, Malmesbury and Bedwyn. The Roman road would now be used by traders, pilgrims, merchants, pedlars, monks. After the confusion and unrest of the early Saxon era, order was established. The passing of the seasons, in rural areas, became the measure and dominant influence on life. The eleventh century dawned – before its end, there would be another change.

Ansfrid holds Bachentune of Gilbert. Edric held it in the time of King Edward, and it paid geld for two hides. There is land for three ploughs. Of this there is one hide in demesne and there are two ploughs, and there are 4 villeins and 7 bordars and 3 cottars with 2 ploughs. There are 8 acres of meadow and 40 acres of pasture. It was and is worth £6.

There was a detached, but tithable part of Beckhampton at Stanmore, south of Clyffe Pypard. There was a village or farmstead there until the sixteenth century; today the only trace of it is a small copse of that name. It was held by the same man:

Ansfrid holds Stanmere of Gilbert. Bruning held it in the time of King Edward, and it paid geld for 2 and a half hides. There is land for two ploughs. Of this there are in demesne 2 hides and there is one plough and 2 serfs; and there is 1 villein and 3 bordars with half a plough. It was worth 20s. It is now worth 40s.

The Normans have arrived and are soon imposing their rule upon the country. The Battle of Hastings has been fought; William is on the throne. We can be grateful to him for providing us with a record of settlements throughout the country in the form of the Domesday Book. It tells us that Beckhampton had 'land for three ploughs' and several small landowners: villeins and bordars both owned land, the latter less than the former. Cottars were cottagers, often without land. A hide is about 120 acres, and one plough team would consist of 8 oxen, jointly owned by the landowners. The proportion of meadow to pasture suggests that the main interest lay in sheep-rearing. Thus we have a sizeable settlement with a good source of income.

It is often thought that the Normans brought culture and learning to the country, mainly because of the many beautiful churches and cathedrals which survive from that era. In fact the opposite is true: the Saxons were more advanced artistically than the Normans, as we have seen; the level of scholarship declined after the Norman Conquest – a regrettable circumstance. Norman building was quite plain at first; during the twelfth century some decorated stonework made its tentative appearance – the earliest recorded use of the typical rounded Norman arches with 'zig zag' mouldings was in Durham Cathedral c1130. Thereafter the pace quickened, stonemasons became more and more adventurous, including flowers and foliage, beasts and men in their work.

In order to dominate the country the Normans set about building – mostly castles in the first place; those in Hastings and Pevensey were begun soon after 1066. As they spread through the country more castles were built, usually of the 'motte and bailey' type – that is a high mound or 'motte' topped by a wooden building and set in an area surrounded by a stockade and ditch – the 'bailey'. These castles were often re-built in stone later on.

All three local towns built castles in medieval times. That of Calne has left no trace other than the names of 'Castle House' and 'Castle Street', which merely suggest an earlier building. Marlborough castle was built by 1070. The motte upon which it was situated is in the grounds of the College today. It is a stepped hill of concentric circles, comparable with Silbury Hill, built on a possibly Neolithic mound. In medieval times royalty stayed there several times, but the castle fell into disrepair, and was a ruin by the fourteenth century.

At Devizes, there was a motte and bailey castle built by Osmund, Bishop of Salisbury, in 1080. The site was at the meeting of three manors: Potterne, Cannings and Rowde, and was known as 'castrum ad divisas' – the castle at the boundaries – leading to the town's modern name. A notable prisoner held there was Robert, Duke of Normandy, son of William the Conqueror. He was there for twenty years following his unsuccessful bid for the throne. The castle suffered a fate common to many – it was burnt down in 1113.

It fell to Osmund's successor, Roger of Caen, to re-build the castle. Roger had also built castles at Malmesbury and Sherborne; he acquired the royal castle at Old Sarum, enlarging its cathedral. With all this experience it is not surprising that the castle at Devizes was described as 'the finest and most

splendid in Europe'. The medieval town grew
up around the castle – today's roads follow
the outer defences – and was doubtless of
some importance to Beckhampton's
residents.

But the average villein or cottar would
not regard the castle as a thing of beauty.
Norman castles were built to intimidate: they
were a symbol of Authority, hence the
building on hills or mounds. The castle at
Devizes was large; it was high, surrounded
by a deep moat. If it did not strike terror into
the hearts of its observers, at the very least it commanded respect. As the local
prison, it would be feared: penalties could be extreme. For poaching just one
rabbit, (regarded as a delicacy by medieval gentry) a man could be imprisoned or
even executed. Those who entered the castle as prisoners rarely came out again.

As long as they remained law-abiding the residents of Beckhampton
would be free to settle down and get on with their own lives, which, one must
presume, they did, once the Normans had been accepted. But once more the
village was about to be involved in national events: it was the twelfth century,
and Henry I was on the throne.

Henry's only son had been drowned in the White Ship in 1119; his only
other child, Matilda, was not named as his successor upon his death in 1135. His
nephew, Stephen of Blois, claimed the throne by reason of his marriage to one
of William the Conqueror's daughters. The conflict between Stephen and
Matilda is well documented, and continued for ten years. Devizes was in a
strategic position during the anarchy, with Stephen's headquarters in Oxford,
and Matilda relying heavily on her half-brother and staunch supporter, Robert of
Gloucester. The castle saw much action during the unrest.

In 1139 Stephen arrested and imprisoned Bishop Roger, among others, at
Oxford. One of the prisoners escaped, and made his way to Devizes castle to join
Matilda of Ramsbury, Roger's mistress. Stephen rode to the castle, taking Roger
and his son as hostages. He had a gibbet erected outside the castle, and paraded
his hostages, the younger Roger with a rope round his neck. Within three days
the castle surrendered, and remained in Stephen's hands for some time. Bishop
Roger was released: all his considerable lands and possessions went to Stephen.

A Greek proverb states: 'When bullocks fight in the marsh it is the frogs
that suffer'. And so the poor 'frogs' of Beckhampton and particularly the little

medieval town of Devizes had to put up with the ravages of this war that was not a war. Crops were destroyed, houses pillaged; in general it must have been a miserable time for the onlookers. The whole country was affected: it was a time often referred to as 'when Christ and His saints slept'. Eventually, the peasants had had enough. 'Simple rustics' besieged the castle and forced Count Hervey, Stephen's son-in-law, to surrender to Matilda. To show her gratitude, Matilda granted the townsfolk freedom from certain tolls; in effect, permission to hold a market. By now she had been proclaimed Queen, but was not well received in London, and was driven out to continue the conflict. In 1141 she was forced to ride from Winchester to Devizes, pursued by Stephen's men. She was said to have ridden 'like a man' – sitting astride for greater speed. She arrived 'more dead than alive', and was sent on to Gloucester for safety.

Thereafter events moved out of the immediate area, and peasants elsewhere became the 'frogs'. In 1145 the battle of Faringdon took place; Stephen won, and Matilda retired to the continent. She sent her son across to try to keep her cause alive, but he was too young to be effective. Perhaps Matilda had named him after his grandfather in the hope that one day he would inherit the throne of England. Her hope was not in vain, for upon Stephen's death in 1154, her son became Henry II.

The whole country must have heaved a sigh of relief that the misery was over; that life could return to normal. Henry would prove to be a good king. One of his many accomplishments was to overhaul the legal system and initiate trial by jury. Yet, sadly, he will probably be best remembered as the king whose Archbishop of Canterbury was murdered following a chance remark.

At the end of the twelfth century we have the first written record of Beckhampton since Domesday. It refers to the chapel of St.Vincent, which was recognised by the parish church of Avebury. Was it newly built, or was it a Saxon chapel? Unfortunately there are no records of its origin. Stukeley mentions the 'old chapel' and 'chapel field' , placing them 'in Bekamton town near the termination of Bekamton Avenue'. A twentieth century archaeologist, O.G.S. Crawford, suggests that the chapel was close to the crossroads, although he gives no reason for his supposition. It is reasonable to infer that the chapel was at the western end of the present village. This is partly borne out by aerial photographs showing hummocks in the fields there, suggestive of medieval occupancy.

The dedication to St.Vincent is unusual in a modern context, although he was a saint of some importance in medieval times. Saint Richard of Chichester, for example, was canonised on St.Vincent's feast day in 1262. Vincent of Saragossa (in Spain) died in 304 AD. He was tortured under the Romans, and relics are claimed in Spain, Portugal and France as well as this country. Six ancient churches are dedicated to him in England. Abingdon, (whose church is dedicated to St.Helen) graded his feast day, 22nd.January, extremely high with an octave or eight-day celebration. The relics there acquired by a twelfth-century monk were doubtless displayed and worshipped. In Burgundy and elsewhere he is patron saint of vine-growers; his feast day giving some protection against early frosts. There is, of course, no explanation as to why Beckhampton's chapel was dedicated to him. He was probably better known in Europe, and it may be that the French monks of Avebury Priory brought news of him. Abingdon is not so far away, and perhaps news of this highly-regarded saint had also spread from there. Both these suppositions lead to the probability that the chapel was medieval rather than Saxon.

Around 1190, the chaplain, Walter, and Asketil, vicar of Avebury, agreed the chapel's status. Walter, and subsequent priests had to make a vow of fidelity to the vicar. Avebury was under the jurisdiction of Cirencester Abbey, but the then Lord of the Manor, Hilary of Beckhampton, also paid tithes to Malmesbury Abbey, therefore a settlement was drawn up, c1190 – 1193, by the abbots of these two houses regarding the use of the chapel.

It was agreed that the villagers were free to attend the chapel at all times. On St.Vincent's feast day everyone, including the Lord of the Manor, should attend the chapel. Hilary and his family should attend the parish church on the four great festivals of Christmas, Easter, Pentecost and Trinity; and for marriages, purifications and baptisms. The chaplain could hear confessions from the manor house, and should receive all dues from Beckhampton except offerings from Hilary at marriages and baptisms. Hilary was also ordered to render two acres of corn yearly to Avebury church.

We have thus a tantalising half picture of medieval Beckhampton, with Hilary, its lord, at the end of the twelfth century. Its position in the parish of Avebury has been established. It has already seen much strife, but for the next few centuries life will be rather more peaceful.

THE THIRTEENTH-CENTURY lord of the manor of Beckhampton was Hamo or Hamon, Knight. In 1235 he appears to have defaulted in his dues to Cirencester Abbey. He was duly reprimanded by a triumvirate of papal judges-delegate: the priors of Winchcombe and St.Oswalds, Gloucester, and the Archdeacon of Gloucester, after which he promised to pay specified tithes to the church at Avebury. He seems to have mended his ways, for in 1236 he was appointed one of four local justices. He is also recorded as having made a gift to St.Nicholas' hospital in Salisbury. Perhaps on his visits to Salisbury he was able to see the new cathedral being built, although he would not have seen its completion.

In the early fourteenth century the manor of Beckhampton was split into two halves, for each of which the judicial term was a moiety. The advowson, or right to appoint priests, descended with the owners of the moieties, a plan of which appears elsewhere.

No doubt the splitting of the manor would have caused some upheaval to the villagers, who must have been divided between the moieties. But the main business of farming the land and raising sheep would have continued; the two landowners collecting their dues and paying their tithes. It is likely that wool was sold in the local towns. The wool trade was of prime importance in Calne; one of the earliest known fulling mills was erected at Stanley Abbey (a small Cistercian abbey between Calne and Chippenham which today exists only as a

small ruin). Marlborough and Devizes were producing cloth at the time. Marlborough's was a rather rough cloth known as 'Burel' or 'Burrell'; its use would eventually die out. A dyer was recorded in Devizes in 1281; by 1315 the town was exporting fine woollen cloth to France. Although Devizes seems to have suffered a general economic decline in the fourteenth century, the wool trade was growing, its merchants becoming rich.

The villagers, in common with all peasantry, would have received little benefit from the flourishing wool trade. Medieval life was governed by the seasons and the church year, into which the agricultural cycle fitted: a life of almost ceaseless toil. But there were compensations – the four great church festivals were times of feasting in which even the peasants shared – having worked twice as hard in order to prepare the food. The downside of these feasts was the preceding fasts. Peasants were not exempt from these, but as their intake of meat was minimal anyway, the lack of it would not have been too onerous.

The year was marked by various religious or secular celebrations, many of which survive today. The first of these was Plough Monday – the first Monday of the New Year. The land was blessed, then ploughed and sown, should the weather permit. Ascension and Pentecost were associated with beating parish boundaries. May Day has given rise to many pagan celebrations throughout the country, latterly with political connotations. Rogation Days were times of blessing the crops. In June, sheep shearing festivals would take place, and a shearing feast held – surely one of the highlights of the year for our villagers. The observance of Midsummer was another pagan rite, then in August Lammas or loaf mass, commemorated the first bread of the new harvest. Then as now, the long season of Trinity culminated in the fast of Advent followed by Christmas and the New Year. No town or village would recognise all these festivals, but they would have provided several welcome breaks from the monotony of day-to-day existence.

As well as celebrations linked to the calendar, there were fairs to look forward to. From the thirteenth century, Marlborough seems to have had a plethora. In 1204 King John granted an eight-day fair to begin on the Eve of the Assumption (August 14th). Over the years it was held later in August, and became agricultural in style. In 1931 Marlborough Fair, Sheep Fair or Great Sheep Fair was held on the Common on August 22nd. It existed until the 1960s. In 1229 King Henry III granted a four-day fair to begin on the Eve of St.Martin (November 10th). This fair's date also moved to later in the month: from the eighteenth century it was held, on the Green, on November 22nd. In 1929 it moved to the Common, and again became an agricultural fair, although in this case sheep are not specified. It was still held in 1938, but, like its predecessor, lapsed in the 1960s. In 1246 King Henry III granted a four-day fair to begin on the Eve of St.Peter and St.Paul (June 28th). This was chiefly a horse fair by the early eighteenth century, and from 1782 was held on July 10th. This fair lapsed much earlier than the previous two; it was held in 1875, but not by 1879. In all probability, this reflected the decline of the coaching trade.

Hiring or Mop fairs were held in the early nineteenth century, and mixed business with pleasure. Little Mop and Big Mop fairs were held on the Saturday before and the Saturday after October 10th, regarded as Michaelmas Day, although today this feast takes place in late September. This tradition is still observed, to the equal fury of motorists and high street traders, who have to contend with the closure of High Street. It need hardly be stated that the purpose, today, is purely for pleasure. The villagers of Beckhampton would surely be permitted to attend one, if not all of these fairs – as long as they could work out when and where they were held!

Although medieval life had its lighter side, the fourteenth century was not a good one for rural areas. Sheep flocks had expanded enormously, supplying the wool industries in the local towns. But the years 1315 – 1322 were disastrous for landowner and peasant alike. The summer of 1315 was marked by bad weather, leading to poor harvests, and murrain among sheep. (Murrain was not a specific ailment, rather a generic term for any infectious disease of cattle – i.e. all livestock. Today's equivalent would be foot and mouth disease.) The next two years also yielded poor harvests, and during the following five years cattle and sheep suffered destructive diseases. Things must have looked very black during these years. But the weather improved; the animals recovered, flocks and herds were built up again. Sadly, worse was to follow with the arrival of the Black Death in 1348. We have no record of how Beckhampton fared during this disastrous era, but the decline in population when the plague had wreaked its havoc led to less demand for corn. To balance this, and much to Beckhampton's benefit, the expanding cloth industry meant that there was more demand, and therefore higher prices, for wool.

The village had survived much during its already long history, and its ability to survive would hold it in good stead for the years to come. In 1334 Beckhampton was assessed at 39s. for taxation. By 1377 there were 31 poll tax payers, and 134 in Avebury. The parish was thriving, and would do so throughout the next century.

Little of note seems to have been recorded at Beckhampton during the fifteenth century. It was a violent and turbulent age with the start of the Hundred Years' War and the Wars of the Roses. Salisbury experienced a brief notoriety in 1483 when the Duke of Buckingham was executed in the market place for his part in the unsuccessful rebellion following the murder – or should one say the disappearance – of the Princes in the Tower. Beckhampton was not concerned with these matters. Rural life continued at its own pace, and while the hierarchy agonised over the ruling factions, country dwellers were concerned with the growing of crops and the herding of beasts; and all their related problems. The village's priority remained agriculture, and particularly sheep.

At the very end of the century, in 1499, a fair was granted on 'Charlborough Down' by Wansdyke. This is part of the escarpment overlooking Pewsey Vale, and is about two miles due south of Beckhampton. Later on the down became known as St.Anne's Hill: the fair took place on August 6th and 7th: the eve of and the saint's feast day. There was and is some controversy about the origin of the name, which may have derived from St.Anne's Chapel, either at

 Allington or All Cannings church. Be that as it may, the fair survived until the twentieth century, and will be dealt with more fully anon. St.Anne's Hill became corrupted to Tan Hill, the name which it and the escarpment bear today. We can be sure that our villagers looked forward to the fair, whose main purpose over the centuries was the trading of sheep.

It is perhaps relevant here to mention the many different spellings of Beckhampton over the years, since with the advent of many written documents it name was becoming standardised. As we have seen, in 1086 it was 'Bachentune'. Over the next three centuries the second two syllables have varied a little: am, an, amp, and ton , tun; the first syllable had ended with 'ch' or 'k' but was always spelt with an 'a'. Scholars differ in their interpretation of its meaning. Some say it could mean Bacca's or Bucca's farmstead. In Old English it would have been *baec-hean-tun*, or settlement by the high back or ridge. There is no obvious ridge in Beckhampton, although the land rises on both sides of the village. Yet others suggest that 'baec' could mean a small stream. (This compares with current usage – in Yorkshire all small streams are becks.) A consensus of opinion seems to point to a home or farmstead, (the 'ham' or 'tun' bit) which might be near a ridge, or have belonged to a man named Bacca. It is tempting to believe the latter – the words are of Saxon origin, and perhaps Bacca was our Saxon thane. In any case, the words originated long before Domesday, and are further evidence of the continuous occupation of the village.

THE SIXTEENTH CENTURY DAWNED; with it the Tudor dynasty, which had come into being with Henry VII in 1485, was consolidated. This era led to some turmoil in royal circles, and religious unrest during the reign of Henry VIII. With the accession of Elizabeth I, in 1558, national events settled down.

The transition from late Medieval to Tudor would have had little impact upon Beckhampton. The two moieties continued, as doubtless did day-to-day life, in much the same manner, with church and agriculture the dominating factors. But there was to be a change within the village.

The chapel had had several priests during the fifteenth century, who may or may not have been residents. In the sixteenth century just two names survive. At its dissolution the chapel estate was valued at £4.8s; it passed to the Crown. In 1549, King Edward VI granted it to John Warner, the current chaplain. Warner sold it in 1561 to Thomas Browne, who may have been related to Francis Browne, patron of the chapel in 1532. John Warner had been appointed by William Button, whose family were Lords of the Manor of Alton Priors from the thirteenth to the seventeenth century; William Button was MP for Chippenham and Marlborough.

John Warner, the last incumbent of the chapel, was appointed in 1544. It is unlikely that he ever set foot in Beckhampton, since he was an eminent theologian and scholar, with other interests throughout the country. A one-time warden of All Souls, Oxford, he held several other university posts. He held canonries in St.Pauls, London, Winchester, Salisbury, Canterbury and Lincoln, together with many rectories. He was chaplain to both Henry VIII and Edward VI. Beckhampton does not receive even a mention in his biographical details held at All Souls. He died in 1565, in London.

Although the Button Family retained their moiety until 1596, no other chaplain was appointed. The owners of the other moiety were in Hertfordshire at the time, and were probably unaware either of the departure of John Warner or of their responsibility in the matter. The Button moiety went to the Trusloe family, who also acquired the chapel estate. Nothing more is known of the chapel itself. It may have been in a bad state of repair by now: many churches in Wiltshire were neglected in the sixteenth century. During this time residents of Stanmore continued to bury their dead in the churchyard, although they would have passed four other burial grounds on the way. By the seventeenth century the chapel was in ruins, and the Trusloe family doubtless put the land to better use.

The chapel would have played an important part in village life during medieval times: its demise may have been gradual. Or the religious unrest during Henry VIII's reign, with its changes of doctrine, may have been the last nail in its coffin. Those who wished to worship would have to go to Avebury from now on.

By the end of the century the village contained some wealthy residents – its tax assessment in 1576 of £9.11s.8d. was higher than that of Avebury. We have no record of these residents, but it is likely that they were wool merchants; sheep farming remained the most lucrative occupation in Beckhampton, and the cloth trade in Devizes increased during this time. In 1599 Thomas Goddard's moiety was said to include mills, although no further reference to them has been found. It is doubtful if the small stream which flowed through the village would have provided enough power for mills. In spite of this, the end of the sixteenth century was surely an affluent time for the village. Sadly, it was not to last.

The rise of gentry families during the sixteenth century meant that the area now known as Wessex was dominated by great estates. Most farmers were tenants, which in turn meant that farm workers – who probably made up the bulk of Beckhampton's population – lived in poverty. Wheat and barley were the main crops; these were dependent on flocks of sheep to fertilise the soil. The sheep were the forerunners of what became the 'Wilts. and Dorset Horn' breeds. They were sturdy animals, bred for their ability to walk from pasture to fields at night, where they were folded with hurdles made from hazel. The hurdles would be moved daily to ensure that the whole field was covered. Most of the tenant's sheep would be kept in a single, large flock, presided over by a shepherd appointed and paid by the tenants. His wages – 6/- per week in 1793 – were supplemented by a great coat yearly, and breakfast on a Sunday. His dog would be his own responsibility.

Around the middle of the century there was an important development in sheep-rearing: the use of water meadows. Villages in the Kennet valley would benefit enormously from the system. The idea was that channels were built so that meadows on either side of a stream or river would be flooded with moving water during the winter months, and would not freeze. The lime-rich water would deposit silt which was beneficial to the pasture. The design and maintenance of these meadows demanded enormous skill. It was essential that the water was kept moving, otherwise it would kill the grass. The 'waterman' or 'drowner' became a figure of much importance: he it was who designed the hatches, weirs and trenches which would control the river's flow, on him depended the success of the meadows. With the coming of spring the floods would be drained away; on the enriched soil grass would grow earlier than on the downs, providing much needed sustenance for ewes and lambs, for whom winter feeds had probably run out. The system meant that larger flocks of sheep could be maintained during the winter months. Later on these meadows would provide an abundance of hay – equally important to sheep farmers. The use of water meadows thrived until the nineteenth century, when a combination of the decline of sheep flocks with improved fertilisers and strains of grasses reduced the need for them. Today they still exist, but on an aesthetic basis rather than a practical one. Salisbury is an excellent example of this. Those in the Kennet valley still flood, thereby saving Marlborough from the threat of inundation; so perhaps they still have some practical value after all.

This development would have caused but a few ripples in the smooth pool of rural life, but the pendulum, locally and nationally, was swinging the other way. Civil War raised its ugly head, and thanks to its proximity to Devizes, Beckhampton, for the third time, found itself in the firing line of the country's strife.

There were many similarities to the earlier conflict of Stephen and Matilda. The south-west was largely Royalist in its sympathies: Charles I's headquarters were at Oxford, as Stephen's had been. Once more Devizes occupied a strategic position. Matters came to a head, locally, with the Battle of Roundway. Although insignificant in the overall action of the War, Roundway was a decisive victory for the Royalists, leading to the greater prize of Bristol. The leaders of the two forces were former acquaintances Sir William Waller, Parliamentarian, and Sir Ralph Hopton, Royalist. With notable foresight, Waller had written to Hopton before their first battle, expressing his sadness and 'with what a perfect hatred I detest this warr without an enimie...'

They had met and fought at the Battle of Lansdown, at Bath, on July 5th, 1643. The result was indecisive: the Royalists won, but lost several key men. They were further demoralised the next day when a powder magazine exploded, injuring and temporarily blinding Hopton. They made for Devizes, so that Hopton could rest and recover, pursued by Waller's men. The castle was dilapidated at this time, and barricades were set up in the town. Hopton reached the safety of the castle, while Waller set up camp near Roundway village. He was lucky enough to intercept a party of Royalists coming from Oxford with much needed supplies of arms. The attack took place at Beckhampton: 200 prisoners and 15 loads of ammunition were taken. How the villagers fared may only be imagined. Perhaps they were initially impressed by the Royalist troops, with their flamboyant dress: brightly coloured tunics, lace collars and feathered hats. But no doubt the village suffered; this war, like the others, took its toll of rural areas. (After the attack, at least one cannon ball rolled away, to be found 350 years later, when a cottage in the village was having an extension built.)

This loss of arms was a setback for the Royalists, who sent the Marquis of Hertford to Oxford to fetch further supplies. Meanwhile Waller set up his guns and attacked Devizes: 'day and night poured great and small shott into us'. This would have been terrifying for the townsfolk, and none too comforting for the villagers of Beckhampton, who must have listened to the bombardment with some trepidation. Waller demanded the surrender of the castle, but Hopton held out, in the expectation of Hertford's return. On the 13th, July, Waller took his men to the downs, his scouts having informed him of the Royalist force returning from Oxford with reinforcements. Hertford fired a gun to signal his return, but Hopton's men misinterpreted this, and they remained in the castle. Thus the Royalists were taken by surprise and outnumbered at the start of the battle.

In spite of this, the initial Parliamentarian attack was repulsed; the Royalists capturing enemy cannon. The Royalists now drew the enemy's fire, then attacked, scattering the Parliamentarian cavalry, and driving them over the edge of the steep, 300ft high escarpment around Oliver's Castle. Standing there today one can feel only horror at the thought of men and horses alike falling to their deaths into what became known as the 'bloody ditch'. Meanwhile, Hopton and his men had emerged from the castle, and soon put paid to the Parliamentarian infantry, whose spirit was undoubtedly broken by the carnage before them.

The tragic setting of the bloody ditch on Roundway Hill

Roundway marked a high point for the Royalists. Devizes remained under Royalist control; Charles had the castle re-fortified, and it remained in his hands until 1645. In September of that year, Cromwell set up another bombardment of the castle. The villagers of Beckhampton would have watched the passage of the army, rather more drably dressed on this occasion, and no doubt again heard the guns raging. The garrison was no match for the ten guns in the market place, and this time the castle surrendered. The parliamentary defeat at Roundway was avenged. It was the beginning of the end for Devizes castle. In 1648 it was 'slighted' by a parliamentary order two years previously: by the early eighteenth century Stukeley wrote, ' the castle is ignobly mangled', and that local people were removing stone for their own buildings.

Meanwhile, in another similarity to the Stephen and Matilda anarchy, ordinary people, (although not in the Devizes area) having suffered once more the effects of battle in their area, were showing their displeasure and anger at the destruction of their land, housing and way of life. They formed a band, in 1645, known as the 'Clubmen'. They consisted of farmers, craftsmen, tradesmen, labourers – the frogs once more protesting to the bullocks. They were neutral, having no sympathy for either of the protagonists; concerned only with protecting their property. Not surprisingly, they had no overall influence on the war; but in any case the main focus of events moved elsewhere until the Battle of Naseby later that year more or less resolved the matter.

The battles may have ceased, but the Puritan way of life now generally imposed must have given little joy to ordinary people. We have seen the importance of church and secular festivals on rural life: now there was little relief from daily toil, with celebrations and merry-making virtually banned. But the largely Royalist south-west was having none of this. The Quaker movement rose in Marlborough and Devizes, and there was opposition in the Church of England to the banning of religious festivals such as Christmas and Easter. There is evidence that country fairs continued to flourish: these were necessary to the rural way of life both as social and commercial occasions. At Woodborough in Pewsey Vale, in 1652, a 'lewd company' gathered from surrounding villages processed to Pewsey where they 'very disorderly danced the morris-dance'. Tan Hill fair continued, giving excuses for the brewing of ale, which sold for at least a month either side of the fair, with all classes of society buying. In all probability the years of the Interregnum were not too onerous for Beckhampton residents, although they doubtless welcomed the Restoration in 1660. With the conflict of war and the uncertainty of the Protectorate over, the village could turn to re-building its resources.

It looks as if these were few. It would take Devizes time to re-build its trading; Marlborough had suffered a major fire in 1653, and its cloth industry was declining. Calne, being off the major routes and having no castle, suffered only one minor skirmish during the war. Yet its wool trade, too, suffered a depression due to the privations of the war. Thus all the village's nearest market towns were running well below par. But, as we have seen, Beckhampton is a survivor.

The Waggon and Horses

There must have been some local excitement in 1663 when the author, John Aubrey, accompanied Charles II to the top of Silbury Hill. And there was still enough life in the village to merit the building of a public house in 1669. Known at first as the 'Bear', it had land enough for resting cattle on their way to London markets, and trade enough for it to survive. By 1724 it had become the 'Hare and Hounds'; today it is the Waggon and Horses. Built of sarsen, and much changed over the years, it is an attractive feature of the present village. It was, and still is, a source of comfort and pleasure for visitors and local people alike.

I F THE SEVENTEENTH CENTURY saw the gradual decline of the village, the eighteenth century would bring about its renaissance.

In 1702, a significant event occurred: after exactly four hundred years, the two moieties united. They were bought by a Charles Tooker, who in turn sold them to Sir Richard Holford in 1710. The estate remained in the Holford family (who were lords of the Manor of Avebury; one of the family founded the arboretum at Westonbirt) until the late nineteenth century, when Sam Darling bought it. A portion of one of the moieties was sold separately in 1638; this was sold on several times until it, too, came into the possession of Sam Darling. The changes of ownership would not affect the workers in the village; farming remained, for the time being, the main source of income.

In 1756 an agreement was drawn up between farmers in Avebury and Beckhampton about working hours. From February to November the employees would work a twelve-hour day from 6a.m. to 6p.m., with two hour-long breaks at 10a.m. and 3p.m. From November to February they would work in daylight hours, with one break from 11a.m. until 12 noon. We have no record of their wages, or whether overtime could be worked; but rising for 6a.m. in February and March cannot have been pleasant, and by November there must have been much work taking place in poor light.

A report by O.G.S. Crawford, (an eminent archaeologist who pioneered work with aerial photography) writing in 1921, suggests that in 1724 there were only four houses in Beckhampton. This seems unlikely, in spite of the inauspicious circumstances of the previous century. Crawford appeared to base his opinion on one of Stukeley's drawings. This is a view from the end of Beckhampton Avenue showing its course from Avebury, and is dated July 19th.1723. Silbury Hill is in the middle distance, and beyond that, the 'serpent's head'. In front of Silbury there are trees within which lurk four rather stylised drawings of houses – certainly not an authentic view of the village, but rather an addition to the aesthetic value of the scene. Stukeley himself, during his visits to the area, refers to 'Bekamton town'. In his day this could have meant a hamlet, or division of a parish. But with three sizeable farms plus the chapel estate, there would surely have been need for more than four houses? On Andrews and

Dury's map of 1773, dwellings are shown on both sides of the present lane. It seems that, to the casual observer, then as now, most of the village was hidden.

Stukeley spent much time in the early part of the eighteenth century visiting not only the major monuments of Avebury, Silbury and Stonehenge, but exploring barrows and stone circles no longer in existence. He was interested in Beckhampton stone avenue, and traced its length to a conclusion, as he thought, near the present Devizes road. Sir Richard Colt Hoare, who lived at Stourhead towards the end of the century, and recorded much of his county in his book 'Ancient Wiltshire', described the avenue as descending towards the Roman road where 'in a low valley it terminates, near a fine group of barrows, under Cherhill Hill, in the way to Oldbury Camp. This point, facing that group of barrows, and looking up the hill, is a most solemn and awful place'. Hoare thought the end of the avenue narrowed (Stukeley called it the Serpent's Tail) – he averred that there was no temple or circle as at the end of the West Kennet avenue, as local people would have remembered it.

Recent excavation by the aforementioned combined universities group has disproved both these gentlemen's theories, although neither was completely wrong. It now seems that Beckhampton stone avenue terminates at the Longstones Cove; there is no sign of stone sockets, destruction pits or burial pits on the line of the avenue beyond this point. Stukeley probably misread the many stones which would have been lying in the area at the time: he wanted to believe in his vision of the Serpent's Tail. Hoare's description could have been accurate:

Longstones Field, the end of the Beckhampton Avenue, with the stones Adam and Eve
against Windmill Hill

from the Cove the 'fine group of barrows' could refer to the Bronze Age cemetery, Longstones long barrow, and the splendid barrows which now lie on either side of the Grange. The high ground near Cherhill appears in the distance from this point.

The end of the avenue has been established, but mysteries remain. A short portion of a ditch was revealed in the southern corner of Longstones field. It had been filled and re-cut several times, indicating some importance in the landscape. The most probable explanation is that of a boundary, perhaps between the area enclosed by the two avenues, and the field system that was developing to the west. There are several single buried stones nearby which may or may not have occurred naturally: one at least is associated with the avenue, others with Longstones long barrow.

Perhaps the most significant recent discovery is that the line of the West Kennet stone avenue appears to be broken just north of New Cottages at the side of the present A4. As the avenue is set in a direct line towards the Sanctuary, it has always been assumed that it was unbroken. Does the break, shortening the Kennet avenue, indicate a closer relationship with Beckhampton Avenue? Although the latter is curved, and the former straight, between them lies Silbury Hill, forming a rough triangle with Avebury at the apex. There are still many questions to be answered about the monuments themselves, and the many ditches and enclosures which formed our ancient landscape.

In Stukeley's time both stone avenues were more or less complete, although he was saddened to record the destruction of stones in Beckhampton avenue. We have his first-hand account of how the stones were felled. First, a pit was dug and filled with straw beside the doomed stone; which was then toppled over the pit. The straw was fired, and when the stone was hot, cold water was poured over it; sledgehammers completed its demise. As he watched, twenty cartloads of stone were taken to build an extension to the Hare and Hounds. We may be sure that many sarsen walls and buildings in the parish were originally part of Beckhampton avenue. 'Farmer Green' appears to be the chief culprit in what would be condemned today as an act of vandalism, yet he was merely making use of a 'natural' resource – in the eighteenth century there was no respect for or preservation of ancient monuments. (The practice of firing stones has continued: Joan Hues, who still lives in the village, noted this procedure when the meadow to the south of the present lane was being levelled out in the 1950s.)

This century, however, was to see a radical change in some of the villager's lives. With the unification of the moieties the proportion of arable to pasture remained more or less the same. Sheep continued to provide the bulk of the income. In 1720 tax assessments suggested that tenant farmers were flourishing, but the demand for wool was decreasing. In Calne the woollen trade continued to flourish, but it had declined in Marlborough, and although new types of cloth were being produced in Devizes, and a new factory built, its owner went bankrupt at the end of the century. Generally, for sheep farmers, the local outlook was not good and the village must have been at a low ebb. But Beckhampton, alone among other villages in the area, had the great good fortune to be situated on what became known as the Great Bath Road; not just on the road, but at an important junction.

As early as 1668, Samuel Pepys travelled from Bath to London. He crossed the downs with some trepidation, apparently worried that the coachman might lose his way. His worries were far from groundless: there were few tracks, no signposts – just large expanses of unmarked downland. He observed that the life of shepherds was 'pretty', 'in fair weather only'. He stopped at Avebury in the afternoon, and was duly impressed by the stone circles and ditches, and also with Silbury Hill. Continuing his journey, he was amazed to see great stones, 'so thick as to cover the ground'. He reached Marlborough before nightfall. Even then, he records five coaches that day on the same route. At the turn of the century Bath became a fashionable spa town; traffic between it and London increased. The road between Shepherd's Shore and Sandy Lane was one of the first to be turnpiked in 1713.

Journeys during those early coaching days were far from comfortable, although the novelty of travel must have compensated a little. To the villagers, the coaches must soon have become a commonplace sight – and sound: by all accounts coach horns were used with great enthusiasm. At first, the Bath road followed the path of the present Devizes road, then through Sandy Lane towards Melksham. But a speedier route was sought, and a more direct road over Cherhill Down and on to Calne and Chippenham was built; this was completed in 1745. There was competition between the two roads at first, and a little sharp practice, leading to the following announcement in the *Bath Journal* of May 12th,1746:

> New Road from Bath to London through Chippenham, Wiltshire.
> Whereas it has been found that the two Turnpike Keepers of Beckhampton near Marlborough and Pickwick near Corsham has falsely and maliciously represented this road as being in bad condition and greatly inferior to that of Sandy Lane. This is to inform the Publick that this road aforesaid is in the best Repair immaginable

and Gentlemen who have not already travelled it are desired to judge for themselves and continue or discontinue its use as they shall find it to excel or be inferior to the other road.

For whatever reason, the new road was deemed to be the better one, and the Sandy Lane route gradually fell into disuse until it was abandoned as a coach route in 1755.

The road from Marlborough to Beckhampton, and the two branch roads beyond, were turnpiked in 1743. Two years later the house which still stands at the cross roads was built as a coaching inn. Built by the owner of the Catherine Wheel Inn at Avebury, it took the same name at first, but was known as the Beckhampton House Inn by 1796. These must have been exciting times in the village, and no doubt its residents were grateful for an extra source of income.

Milestone, Devizes side of Beckhampton

Coaching, of course, could be extremely hazardous, especially during the winter months. Coachmen and passengers alike had to contend with rain, snow and high winds – the latter a particular danger on top of Cherhill. More than once villagers have toiled up the hill to rescue the occupants of an overturned coach, sometimes, sadly, arriving too late to save the lives of horses or travellers. Eventually a new road was built below the brow of the hill, just about where the A4 runs today, but this was not opened until the end of the century.

Another, less expected hazard was the stone avenue. Running alongside the road in places, it could cause the horses to shy, and the Turnpike Trustees ordered certain stones to be removed. It is easy to imagine the effect on the horses – perhaps on a moonlit night – of enormous sarsens suddenly looming beside the road.

Then there were the highwaymen. One of the most notorious gangs operated near Beckhampton – the Cherhill gang. Despite the erection of a gibbet on the Calne road, on which some of their number were hanged, they carried out their robberies for some years. As the gibbet was fairly isolated, the gang could climb up and remove the body of their dead colleague at night. This practice ceased when the authorities bound the gibbet post with iron, tarred it and drove in nails. The gang, however, were not deterred from their activities. They were not above attacking those who had helped them: a barrister called Sergeant Merryweather was robbed one evening by the man for whom he had gained an acquittal that morning – irony indeed. They were said to have carried out their raids naked – surely in the summer months? One would like to think that Beckhampton men had nothing to do with such reprobates, but there is no proof either way, and the life of a farm labourer is not the most affluent . . .

Perhaps the worst coaching hazard was the road itself. One has only to think today of the damage done to the Ridgeway and other tracks by four-wheel drive vehicles to imagine the state of coaching roads, particularly in winter. The steep descent into Marlborough from Savernake was notoriously difficult, and the scene of many an accident. In 1753 Parliament brought in the 'Broad Wheel Act' which required wagons to have wheels of not less than 9 inches wide, in order to flatten and compact the surface rather than churn it up. This problem was never really resolved, and passengers had to make the best of the uneven roads.

In spite of the disadvantages, people were still attracted to Bath; among them Charles Dickens. Opinions differ about whether the inn mentioned in the Bagman's Story in 'Pickwick Papers' is based on the Waggon and Horses: as it was referred to as 'about half a quarter of a mile from the end of the Downs' a more likely candidate seems to be the inn that was at Shepherd's Shore. Dickens undoubtedly stayed in Beckhampton: as late as 1977 the story of the 'talking chair' (also in the Bagman's story: in which a strange chair comes to life and converses with the storyteller) was associated with the Waggon & Horses. There is some controversy, too, about the origin of the title of 'Pickwick Papers': the book could have been named after the village through which the coach would pass on its way to Bath, or it could have been named after a Bath business man. Moses Pickwick was the owner of Bath to Oxford stage coaches and the White Hart Hotel (later the Grand Pump Room Hotel) in Bath. Sam Weller draws Mr.Pickwick's attention to the name on the side of the coach in which he is travelling, with some scorn, taking offence at the name 'Moses'. But Mr.Pickwick is equable, and accepts the apparent coincidence. As Moses was a descendant of a foundling picked up in the village of Pickwick, who was given the name of the place where he was found, both suppositions can be satisfied. Dickens seemed to draw no inspiration from the Downs since the area hardly features in his books. Then as now Wiltshire is a rather pleasant part of the journey, not the destination.

Although the roads were poor, amenities began to appear. At some roadsides pumps were placed so that the dust could be settled during the summer months. There was even talk of lamps between Marlborough and Shepherd's Shore, but one observer noted somewhat wryly that 'public spirit must have been on the decline since that memorable offer'. In order to settle any arguments as to priority when two coaches met, a system of driving on the left was set up. This was confirmed by the Highways Act of 1835, and is, of course, still observed today. A suggestion then that we drive on the right was not taken up, and thus this country remains out of step with most of the rest of the world in the matter of road use.

The most lasting, and noticeable achievement, was the erection of milestones. These were put up during the 1740s: many of them are still *in situ* today. Although the road would have continued to Bristol, it is Bath that appears on the stones. Different Trusts used different shapes; near Bath cast iron plates were set into the stones.

Milestone, Marlborough to Calne A4

It is some indication of the importance of Beckhampton crossroads that two inns became established. This meant that plenty of labour was needed to care for the travellers and the horses: the villagers had a good source of employment. With the fare from London to Bath at around £1, it is doubtful if the wages of ostlers, chambermaids and the like were much better than those of farm labourers, but at least there was work available.

1776 seems to have been a year of some note. Firstly, the Great Snowstorm occurred – the worst, it is reported, since 1739 – 1740. Drifts of eight to twelve feet were recorded, and the Beckhampton and Marlborough Inns were overflowing with marooned passengers.

Events were moving towards mechanisation in the cloth trade; the first spinning jenny in the west was set up in Shepton Mallet in this year. It was not well received, of course , because its use led to a reduction in the demand for labour. This would not have had a direct influence on our villagers, but was an indication of the way the wind was blowing. There were riots at Bradford-on-Avon over carding machines in 1791, and at Trowbridge over the flying shuttle in 1792. The advent of machinery, combined with competition from the north of

England, spelt the beginning of the end of the woollen industry in the west; but the demand for wool did not cease, and it would be another century before sheep farming in Beckhampton declined.

Nearer to home, 1776 saw the first excavation of Silbury Hill. Under the patronage of the Duke of Northumberland, a Colonel Drax was directed to sink a vertical shaft from the middle of the flat top of the hill to the original ground level – over 100 feet below. The only surviving record of this event is a paragraph in a Bristol newspaper. It states that the shaft was eight feet square at the top, tapering to five by four and a half feet at the base, and that it was dug by miners from Mendip. It seems obvious that the purpose of this excavation was to ascertain whether Silbury Hill was a burial mound: possibly of King Sil himself. In spite of 'great labour bestowed on it', nothing was found.

There was not the interest in archaeology then that there is today, and the goings-on at the hill may have had little effect on the village. Some of the men may have been employed to help with the digging. But the whole thing was probably a nine days' wonder, especially in view of the inconclusive outcome.

Perhaps of more interest to the men was the establishment of a cricket ground on Beckhampton Down. This was situated in the low valley behind the Beckhampton House Inn upon which the gallops are sited today. Beckhampton could not raise its own team, but maybe some of the villagers played for Devizes, Calne or Marlborough, the three towns whose teams used the ground. The first recorded match was in 1774, between Marlborough and Devizes. Marlborough won by 118 runs to 76, in spite of being less favoured. The following year Devizes played both Marlborough and Calne, and won both matches. Their success was not built upon: it would be nearly a century later, in 1850, before Devizes' cricket club was founded. After 1775 there are no more records of games at Beckhampton, yet the ground remained in use. In 1830 a reward of two guineas was offered for information following the theft of a quantity of chain. A poster states that 'The chain had been painted white but the paint was much worn off.' This would suggest that the ground was not particularly well cared-for and probably near the end of its usefulness. In time the land would be put to more profitable use for training racehorses.

Cricket was not the only diversion that would be enjoyed by the villagers. Apart from the medieval fairs already mentioned, on several hill tops in Wiltshire there were revels of one sort or another. On Martinsell, for instance, local youths would slide down the hill using horses' skulls as makeshift sledges. Our residents found their amusement nearer to hand. Colt Hoare records that:

country people meet on top of Silbury Hill every Palm Sunday, when they make
merry with cakes, figs, sugar and water fetched from the swallow head, or spring
of the Kennet.

The practice of using Silbury hill for entertainment continued for well
over a century, by which time Palm Sunday became synonymous with Fig
Sunday. We have an account written in a book published in 1923. The writer
obtained his facts from living people, who had themselves attended the fair in
their youth. He describes stalls on the roads approaching Silbury selling toys,
sweets, nuts, ginger beer, gingerbread cakes – and figs. The fair attracted
hundreds of people from the villages around, dressed in their best, indulging in
'much merry-making and drinking'. The youngsters, as at Martinsell, used to
slide down the hill, using planks, not skulls; 'to the detriment of their nether
garments'. The fair eventually died out c1882, although another book of 1932
mentions that 'children still climb Silbury hill, the only relic of the generally
observed Fig Sunday of 100 years ago'.

Towards the end of the century an exciting development in the coaching
industry took place – the introduction of Royal Mail Coaches. A Bath businessman, John Palmer, had put forward a plan for the speedier transportation of
mail by special coaches, changing horses every six to eight miles. It was two
years before the first trial coach ran, in August, 1784. It was a great success; the
Bath Chronicle recorded that: 'The New Mail Coach has travelled with an
expedition that has been really astonishing, having seldom exceeded 13 hours in
going to or returning from London.' Although there was some opposition from
people not living on the mail route, by 1787 mail coaches were running on all
main routes in England and Scotland. This splendid new service demanded new,
improved coaches. How the villagers must have thrilled to their first sight of these
Royal Mail Coaches: with their black and maroon livery decorated with the royal
arms and stars of the four orders of knighthood, to say nothing of the red wheels.
Four horses were used, the coaches themselves being regularly cleaned and
maintained. Royal Mail Coachman was a job much sought-after and respected.

Such exotic occupations were probably not for our villagers; those not
working in the coaching trade would be employed as farm labourers. There
were changes here, too: agriculture was becoming more of an industry, with
advances in farming techniques and productivity. The Bath and West of
England Society was founded in 1777; from its inception to the present day its
aims have been the encouragement of agricultural development through
shows, meetings, lectures, practical demonstrations and publications. The use

Milestone, Avebury side of Beckhampton

of water meadows remained important in the chalklands; new crops were introduced thanks to greater use of fertilisers. Corn, especially wheat and barley, remained the most profitable; fodder crops such as vetch, turnips, clover and rape were introduced, along with a system of fallowing, usually every third year. Books on the subject of farming began to appear; iron equipment replaced the old wooden tools. The breeding of stock improved: although horses had been used on the lighter chalk soils for some time, new breeds appeared that could cope with heavier clay soils, and the use of oxen died out.

These developments were advantageous to farmers; but their labourers were less well off. Through the eighteenth and nineteenth centuries enclosures took place. This is a complex subject and its effects varied. From medieval times if farm labourers owned land it would have been in small strips. Now the strips were being amalgamated into large fields, so many small tenants would lose their land; arable ground began to take over downland pasture. Worse, for the small tenant, common rights were lost as commons were enclosed. This system made great economical sense for landowners, but meant incredible hardship for already hard-pressed farm workers. The loss of access to commons meant the loss of grazing animals, and thus a great part of their income. To some extent this was offset by a greater need for labour at the end of the century: the Napoleonic Wars ensured a high demand for corn, and, for the moment, the agricultural industry flourished.

This century saw the establishment of two large houses in the village which remain to this day. The Holfords built their farmhouse, and Beckhampton House Inn was built by the crossroads. Both houses had cellars, although Stukeley had observed:

> Bekamton village lies very low, at the bottom of a valley subject to inundations, and the ground is very springy: they can't make cellars there: whereas Abury is very dry, and their wells deep.

Stukeley was right; the cellars still exist, but flood when the water tables rise. The old farmhouse on the site of present-day Willonyx also had a cellar: this is now closed off, and so far the present occupants have not explored the nether regions of their house, in spite of threats from neighbours to rip up the carpets and have a look!

Wiltshire in general was gaining itself a not particularly flattering reputation of being a county of 'country bumpkins', but then poor living conditions do not make for brilliant minds. It was at this time that the 'moonraking' story came into existence. Its origins are uncertain, but the reference is to men raking a pool for what they thought was a cheese, but was in fact a reflection of the full moon. This led to some derision, and the (rather unfair) rhyme: ' Wiltshire born and Wiltshire bred, strong in the arm and thick in the head'. But in 1850 there was a twist in the tale. Some Wiltshire men were raking smuggled brandy kegs from a pond when the excise men passed by and challenged them. The men pretended that they were 'moonraking'; the excise men were deceived, and went on their way. This story is preserved in Edward Slow's poem. 'The Wiltshire Moonrakers'. Links with smuggling may have led to the term 'moonshine', which also came into use at this time.

'Thick in the head' or not, Beckhampton's residents now had two steady sources of income, and did they but know it, the future of the village was assured.

THE NINETEENTH CENTURY was one of general expansion and development throughout the country. The first census was taken in 1801, when there were 99 people living in the village. By 1841 the number of residents had risen to 155: these included a family of six children, the eldest of whom, one Charles Goddard, aged 15, was presumably the breadwinner. We know nothing of the family or why the children were left to fend for themselves. One can only hope that the friendly spirit present in the village today existed then, and that neighbours kept an eye on the young family. There are no separate figures for Beckhampton from 1841: the village was included in Avebury. Here the population rose to a peak of 769 in 1871, declining to 588 in 1901. In general the phenomenon of 'urban drift' became apparent as people were attracted to towns by developing industries and the consequent higher wages. But many towns in Wiltshire experienced a decline in population towards the end of the century;

Calne was one exception due largely to the newly-established Harris's Bacon factory. For the rest, the industrial Midlands attracted many, as did even broader horizons overseas. There would be great changes in all areas before the century was out. When the young queen Victoria came to the throne in 1837, few people would have imagined what the next 60-odd years would bring.

One of the earliest changes took place in Pewsey Vale, when the Kennet and Avon canal was dug, mainly in response to increased demand for coal as the age of machinery grew. The canal was opened for use in 1810. It would have had little influence on life in Beckhampton, but no doubt the villagers were interested in its development. Perhaps some of them walked to Devizes to view what must have been a wonder of engineering: the Caen Hill flight of locks.

In the village, the coaching industry continued to prosper with improvements to the roads, and an ever increasing speed of service in the wake of the Royal Mail. The weather continued to wreak havoc, and at Christmas, 1836 the 'worst snowstorm in coaching history' occurred. Drifts of twelve to fourteen feet were reported on the downs, and lives were lost, human and equine. A contemporary account states that on December 26th there were 'no coaches, nothing moving'. In spite of this, the following day the Duke of Wellington set out from Marlborough to visit Badminton. When he got to Silbury hill and found that the road ahead was closed, local farmers came to his rescue and led him through 'Beckhampton Street'. We must assume that he eventually reached his destination, but were the villagers even aware of the notable presence in their midst?

There is a curious story linked to a grave at the side of the Devizes road, near the Roman road. This grave, marked by stones at the head and foot, has been attributed to various people: a highwayman, a deserter, a suicide, a gypsy, a tramp – in other words the origin was unknown. But in response to a newspaper article in 1950, the following story was told.

In 1811, a Royal Mail coach was attacked by highwaymen. They killed the driver, took some valuables, and made off towards Beckhampton. On the way they met a labourer, William Leader, from Devizes, who was returning home drunk. They stunned him and laid him by the dead driver, with the pistol beside him. He was arrested and tried; the

Milestone, Marlborough Road, A4

evidence was conclusive, and Leader was condemned to death. As he was led to the gallows, (on the site of the old Devizes gaol) he cried that he saw a man approaching on horseback, but fog thickened, and the sentence was carried out. Half an hour later a horseman arrived with a reprieve for Leader: one of the highwaymen had turned king's evidence. Leader's body was buried under the only tree for two miles. His story lived on – in 1880 Mary Goddard, a servant to the Wentworth family, who were tenant farmers of Beckhampton Estate for most of this century, used to talk of a stump of gibbet on which a man was hanged for robbing a coach. She heard they 'hanged the wrong man.'

In 1829 the portion of land which had remained outside the two moieties was bought by Thomas Pinniger. We are fortunate in having his first-hand description of life in Beckhampton through his diaries. His immediate concern was building: a brewhouse, stables, waggon house, and, finally, re-building the farmhouse. This is the house known today as Willonyx; the outhouses were converted in the 1980s to form Silbury Court. It is interesting to trace the buildings back to their source. The foundation of the new house was laid in September, 1829. Some roof tiles and other materials were used from the old house; it is likely that the new house adjoined the old. Timber was fetched from Honeystreet wharf; limestone from Calne was used for the main part of the house; bricks and tiles were brought from Devizes. Stone for the portico and

A view across Beckhampton Lane into Silbury Court

chimneys came from Box. The roof was finished in early December, then building ceased due to poor weather. It was resumed in March,1830. In October, Mr.Pinniger gave the masons a finishing supper, but it was December 4th. before the tradesmen finally left. The Pinniger family remained in Beckhampton until the end of the century. Their relationship with their neighbour, Mr.Wentorth, was mostly friendly, given the odd boundary dispute. The use of new machinery was shared, as were, doubtless, discussions on the weather, crops and livestock.

Those villagers who worked in the coaching industry were assured of employment for the time being, at least. Their farm labouring brothers were less well off. During the Napoleonic Wars wages had risen to a giddy 12s. a week. By 1823 they were back to 7s. a week. The price of a loaf of bread varied: there is an interesting record on the wall of the church at Great Wishford – six miles north-west of Salisbury in the Wylye valley. Stones were set in the wall displaying the cost of loaves so that villagers could see that they were not being overcharged, as bread was particularly expensive in their village. The price per gallon (which oddly reflected the dry ingredients) in 1800 was 3s.4d. This worked out at 10d for a 2lb loaf. The next stone is dated 1801, or more likely, according to a stonemason, 1811, when the price has risen to 11½d. By 1904, the next stone records a huge reduction to 10d a gallon, or 2½d a loaf. (The latest stone, inserted to commemorate the Millennium in 2000, records the price per gallon as £3.72, or 93p a loaf.) Whatever the price of bread, seven shillings a week hardly represents a living wage. Other factors influenced the decrease in wages: the effect of enclosures, changes in farming practice, the decline of the cloth industry in the face of growing competition from the North of England.

William Cobbett contrasted the beauty of the countryside in Wiltshire with the poverty of its inhabitants, during his 'Rural Rides' in 1826. He wrote:

> This is, I verily believe it, the worst used labouring people upon the face of the earth. Dogs and horses are treated with more civility; and as to food and lodging, how gladly would the labourers change with them!

Richard Jefferies also noticed the growing disparity between the rich and the poor. He wrote a letter to *The Times* about the farm labourer in 1872,

> his food may, perhaps, have something to do with the deadened slowness which seems to pervade everything he does – there seems a lack of vitality about him.

Indeed the lot of farm workers was a very bleak one, and would remain so until the First World War created a demand for agricultural products. In the

1870s a series of poor harvests and cold, wet summers led to a general slump. The arrival of steam machinery meant less employment. Matters were made worse by the importation of cheap corn from the USA and Canada: wheat prices fell from 70/- per quarter (i.e. 28lbs: a quarter of a hundredweight) in 1847 to 46/- in 1870 and only 24/- in 1894. (70 shillings is £3.50 in decimal coinage; 28 pounds about 12.7 kilograms.) Arable land was laid to grass, but wool prices were also falling.

The life of agricultural workers was very far from that of jolly, well-fed peasants commonly depicted in nineteenth century paintings. Their mean, cob and thatch dwellings – perhaps hovels would be a better word – contained few possessions. Bread was the main constituent of their diet, with some cheese, potatoes and beer. If they were lucky they might have small quantities of meat and dairy products. Their clothing was barely adequate, especially in winter. Shepherds and herdsmen were provided with long woollen cloaks by their employers; carters and ploughmen would wear linen, wool or canvas smocks over shirt and breeches, with straw or felt hats. Their wives would wear a plain woollen gown over petticoats or shifts, a straw hat and an apron, with a woollen shawl for cold weather. Shoes would be locally produced leather. The growth of industries in towns meant that farmers' wives could no longer earn money through by-products such as spinning, knitting, button and bonnet-making: these items were now mass-produced. The damp, insanitary and over-crowded houses led to diseases such as rheumatism, T.B. and bronchitis. This appalling hardship to families led, in 1830, to riots.

Things came to a head locally when the 'Swing' riots – named after a purely fictional leader, Captain Swing – took place. Agricultural workers destroyed machinery, fearing, rightly, that the new threshing machines would deprive them of work during the winter months. For good measure, they also set fire to barns and ricks. This demonstrates their despair and frustration, for in firing corn they were destroying the provision of their own livelihood. Local farmers and landowners set up a force consisting of specially sworn-in constables. Marlborough became the headquarters for the local group, which was known as the 'Tottenham Association', being under the leadership of the Earl of Cardigan, who lived at Tottenham House near Savernake. Mr.Wentworth of Beckhampton – he was the Holford's farm manager – was sworn in as a special constable. Most of the villages in the Upper Kennet valley took part in the riots, with two exceptions: Lockeridge, where the tenant farmer had left for Australia, taking many men with him; and Avebury, where the main employer was a wealthy Newbury farmer, one George Brown. He allowed his employees to rent allotments, thereby providing them with an additional source of food. Beckhampton, having another source of income, was probably not involved, although we cannot say for certain that none of the farm labourers contributed to the unrest.

Mr.Pinniger played his part. He records various fires, then he joins the Marlborough Troop of Cavalry who were 'scouring the country' on several days, and arresting the rioters. On November 25th he records a much diminished market at Devizes, and we must assume that normal agricultural life had come to a standstill. More prisoners were taken until on November 29th rioters at Bremhill were promised an increase in wages to 10/- a week for winter and 12/- for summer. There are no more entries about the riots, and we do not know whether these rises in pay were ever carried out. The riots lasted for only a fortnight locally, although they spread to neighbouring counties. In Wiltshire, 339 men were arrested; almost half were sentenced to transportation; a third were acquitted. Sadly, the riots achieved little, except perhaps to relieve the feelings of the participants.

This century would see changes in religious attitudes. After the turmoil of the sixteenth and seventeenth centuries, the Church of England, as it now was, was proving less than satisfactory. A possible explanation lies in a survey of Wiltshire in 1783. Of 262 parishes, 124 had incumbents that were non-resident. As we have seen from the demise of our own chapel in the sixteenth century, a non-existent priest does not encourage worship. In general, Protestant nonconformity grew rapidly after the Restoration. Several nonconformist chapels had sprung up in the three local towns: there was also one at Avebury. In 1844 Mary Amor's house in Beckhampton was licensed for dissenters meetings. The duration of this meeting-place is not recorded, or the denomination followed. The parish church at Avebury, being the head of the rural deanery, continued to prosper, so the villagers' spiritual needs, whether church or chapel, were adequately provided for.

There must have been some local excitement in the summer of 1849, when John Merewether, Dean of Hereford and an archaeologist, turned his attentions to Silbury Hill. He doubted whether the shaft sunk by Drax in 1776 had reached the centre of the mound. Rather than re-open this shaft, he and a civil engineer, Henry Blandford, set about driving a horizontal tunnel from the south-western edge to the heart of the hill – a distance of 80+ yards. The tunnel was huge by today's standards: 3 feet wide and, in order to maintain the dignity of the Dean and his engineer, 6 and a half feet high – tall enough to accommodate gentlemen wearing top hats! The shaft went beyond the centre of the hill, but found nothing. Merewether ordered side shafts to be dug: one of these disturbed infilling from the 1776 shaft, but nothing of note. His only interesting observation was that of eight sarsen stones set around the base of the hill. The Dean claimed that he had excavated the 'very core' of Silbury, yet nothing had been discovered. He surmised that 'the purpose of the hill was not sepulchral'.

A few years later, in 1862, the Reverend A.C.Smith. vicar of Yatesbury, declared that it was still possible that an off-centre tomb might be present, but no action was taken. Silbury Hill kept its secrets, and it would be more than a century before another excavation was made.

By now, stirring events were taking place in the world of transport – the coming of the railways. In 1843, Swindon rose as a railway town; locomotive workshops were set up, and the railway village built. The G.W.R. (Great Western Railway – affectionately known as God's Wonderful Railway) pushing ever westwards, opened the London – Bristol line in 1841, having overcome immense problems of landscape, notably the Box tunnel, in the process.

Mr.Pinniger decided to view this new phenomenon for himself, and in May, 1841, he walked through the then unfinished tunnel. He went on to Chippenham, where he witnessed the arrival and departure of London trains. Later, when the line opened in July, he recorded a few statistics. The train travelled from London to Bristol, (120 miles) in four hours. Work on the line had commenced in February, 1836; the original estimate being two and a half millions, the outlay in 1841 being five millions. (An interesting comparison with today's estimates of large-scale engineering work: nothing changes!) The Box Tunnel, nearly three miles long, had taken three years to complete. 'Upwards of 20 millions of bricks' were used at a cost of £200,000.

The tunnel, and the small subsidiary one between Box and Bath, remain today one of the wonders of the G.W.R. , and arguably, one of its beauties in the imposing arches at their entrances. Isambard Kingdom Brunel built his railway 'cathedrals' – especially that of Temple Meads at Bristol, and the people rushed to worship. The novelty and speed of this new form of transport were compelling, and inevitably the coaching trade declined.

Its demise was gradual but assured. People still travelled by coach, but less and less. By 1864 the Marlborough branch line was open, and that year saw the abolition of turnpike gates and bars around London. During the next decade turnpike trusts all over the country were wound up; the coach, as a means of long distance transport, was dead. This had a devastating effect on towns, particularly Marlborough and Calne where the number of coaches per day was

The cross-roads, 1930s, showing Beckhampton House

vastly reduced by 1842. Not only towns, but coaching inns suffered, with consequent lack of employment in the villages. Again, this radical change might have meant the end of the village of Beckhampton, but again, it survived, by another stroke of luck.

This time it was the Beckhampton House Inn that saved the day. Initially built as a coaching inn, sometime during the early part of the century it had become the meeting place of the Beckhampton Club – one of several such clubs consisting of the principal gentry of the area, who met in order to choose parliamentary candidates. Little is known of these clubs, but their existence seems to have been of short duration. The Inn's business as a staging post had fluctuated; it had changed hands several times. Its future was looking uncertain when in 1835 William Treen, a racehorse trainer from the west country, stepped in and bought the Inn, in order to make use of the stables, and the adjoining downs. These, which had been grazed by sheep for centuries, were ideal for gallops, with springy turf providing a smooth yet firm surface.

There was still much interest in horses in the area; racing took place at Marlborough and Roundway Down. The latter was a short-lived affair: races were named after (and presumably sponsored by) local institutions, and included the Beckhampton Inn Stakes, but interest seems to have died out after a few years. William Treen was officially designated a publican, and the Inn remained open to travellers until 1855, when it became a full-time racing stable. It has remained so ever since. Thus Beckhampton survived yet another threat to its security. Those employed in the coaching industry , looking after horses, adapted their skills to the care of racehorses, and the village's source of income remained.

With the coming of the railways, use of the Kennet and Avon canal also declined. The G.W.R. bought it in 1852; it continued to be used, but on a much smaller scale, until by 1910 traffic had virtually ceased. The Waggon and Horses had ceased to be a coaching inn, but remained a profitable business. In 1873 it was sold as part of the Avebury Manor Estate. Then it was a sizeable concern: a relic of the days when it provided shelter for herdsmen and their animals on their way to the London markets. It was described in the sale catalogue as having a bar, bar parlour, sitting room, kitchen, brew house, malt house, four bedrooms and a 'capital garden'. There were also two cow houses and a four-stall stable, and on the opposite side of the road a large coach house with lofts over, a cow house, piggeries and garden. Arable land was included, proclaimed boldly as '5 acres, 3 roods and 29 perches' and in smaller lettering underneath, with Victorian honesty – '(more or less)'.

The second part of the nineteenth century marks the heyday of the Tan Hill fair. A contemporary account of 1920 sets the scene: on top of the hill gypsies encamped to await the fair, while clouds of dust on the lower slopes mark the advent of the herds to be bought and sold. By now the fair takes place on August Bank Holiday Monday – a more convenient date than the traditional St.Anne's Day – August 7th. Some of the flocks (and men) will have travelled all night; by early morning most of the sheep will have been penned to await the sale. Breakfast is taken: a simple meal for the shepherds and shared with their dogs, washed down with some of the vast quantities of beer and cider on sale. Local farmers arrive, some with their families, for now the fair is less of a 'rough and tumble' event than it was during the last century. At one time there were swings and roundabouts for the children. Meanwhile in the large barn which is only opened once a year for this event, a sumptuous lunch is being prepared. All is hustle and bustle as the crowds assemble and await the main event.

At about ten o'clock the auctioneer, in his 'little house on wheels', will start the selling. A drover moves the sheep as various lots are sold; the auctioneer's clerk notes down the details. Tegs, (young sheep) two- four- or six-tooth ewes, wethers (castrated male sheep), lambs; all come 'under the hammer' to the benefit of buyer or seller. All is finished by noon; and the more privileged visitors repair to the barn for lunch. Now it is the turn of the gypsies to introduce some horse-trading. In the heat of the day those who have partaken too freely of strong drink may well be regretting their indulgence. In the early afternoon the long trek homeward (for some) begins. Those who live nearer are free to enjoy the jollity which will extend into the night. Fires are lit – a custom which dates back to pagan days. There are stories of a black cockerel being burnt alive; its ashes used to scour the cattle. The women and children will return home – this is no longer a place for them. As one observer put it, ' no one really knew what went on up the hill.'

The next day the fair would disperse – with men no doubt working under great difficulty and with many a sore head. The sheep are moved on to their new homes; hurdles are stored away in the barn. The gypsies and other followers prepare to move on – for there were many hill-top fairs in Wiltshire. Tan Hill fair lasted until the 1930s: it definitely took place in 1939. After that a combination of the second world war and the difficulties experienced by the lorries and vehicles used to transport the animals up the steep hill led to its demise. During the war it took place at least twice in the fields opposite Silbury hill, but its original site was never used again. The barn has long since disappeared: Tan Hill is now just a point on the map, and has given its name to the escarpment. In the 1930s it appeared on O.S. maps as St.Anne's Hill. At almost 1,000 feet, it is the highest point in Wiltshire, yet it has almost faded into obscurity.

B Y THE END of the century the country as a whole was organising its administrative areas. Local government became increasingly responsible for police and fire services, education, public works, roads, health, housing and welfare. County Councils were set up in 1889, and by 1894 Parish Councils were in existence, as were urban and rural district councils. The boundaries of these new areas existed until 1934, when some parishes were abolished, and six rural districts set up in Wiltshire. Forty years later a further review took place, and five districts were established. One of these, Thamesdown, became

Swindon Borough, which then broke with the county. Beckhampton became part of Kennet District Council, which has earned itself the reputation of being one of the best run district councils in the country.

In 1877 a school in the village was applied for, but the buildings were deemed inadequate. It seems that the venture was not followed up, and then as now, local children attended Avebury school.

By now, newspapers were well established. Our villagers had many choices, and there was no excuse not to be up-to-date with the news. As early as 1736 the *Salisbury and Winchester Journal* was available in all three local towns; it is still available today, but is centred on Salisbury. But the most popular paper would have been the *Devizes and Wiltshire Gazette*, again sold in all three towns. This was established in 1819, and became the *Wiltshire Gazette* in 1909. In 1956 it joined the *Wiltshire Herald and Advertiser* to become the *Wiltshire Gazette and Herald*. This paper is still running, with separate editions for each town available since 1988. Throughout this century other papers came and went, most of them bewilderingly bearing the title 'Gazette', 'Herald' or Advertiser'; all relatively short-lived.

Devizes and Marlborough still have their own papers: the *Devizes News* started in 1979, while Marlborough has its *'Times'*, established in 1859, but not in production from 1910 to 1949; and the *Evening Advertiser*, established in 1898. The *Wiltshire Telegraph* was a great innovation. Published from 1877 to 1933 in Devizes, it was among the first newspapers to use tinted paper, in June 1884. Not surprisingly, it was often referred to as the 'Pink Paper'. After several metamorphoses, it was incorporated into the *Wiltshire Gazette* in 1942, when it doubtless reverted to white paper. Of interest to Beckhampton's residents, perhaps, would have been Marlborough's *North Wiltshire Herald*, established in 1861. This was aimed partly at the farming community, but after two changes of title, it folded in 1956.

In 1897 the War Office purchased large areas of Salisbury Plain – and sheep which had been prevalent for centuries were gone for good. The isolated village of Imber would remain until the second world war, when its residents left voluntarily. They would never return, in spite of promises at the time that their village would be re-occupied. Today it is a sad mixture of a few original buildings and army breeze-block structures.

As the century turned, an event that would prove important for Beckhampton came about. On 8th.March,1882, one Samuel Darling, a racehorse owner and breeder from Heddington, happened to be in Calne to meet his solicitor. He found out that negotiations for the sale of the

Beckhampton stables were going on between the then owner, Harry Woolcott, and a man named Weston. However, Mr. Weston had not turned up, and Sam Darling expressed his interest in the property. Mr. Woolcott's agent, a Mr. Parry, asked if he were prepared to pay a deposit. Sam Darling agreed, and in his own words, 'I gave him a cheque for £500, and Beckhampton was mine'.

Thus, almost by chance, the stables came into the hands of one of its most successful owners. Its fortunes had fluctuated during the previous thirty years. Under Harry Woolcott the Beckhampton-trained filly, 'Formosa' became the first horse in racing history to win four Classics in 1868. Then in 1873 Sir George Chetwynd became principal patron. He was later denounced as a cheat and left racing in 1879. Meanwhile Woolcott's health was failing; the stables were at a very low ebb when Sam Darling bought them. He, and his son Fred, would revive the stables and become highly successful trainers. They were to remain in the village for more than fifty years.

Sam Darling set about extending and improving the stables with the introduction of acetylene gas for lighting, and better drainage. He also improved the living accommodation of the stable hands. Not long after he moved, the stables had a scare. At the time of the great manoeuvres in Wiltshire (before the First World War) 25,000 troops passed through Beckhampton. One of the troopers took a very sick horse into the yard, without permission, and there drenched it. The horse died on the road just over a mile away; the fever from it was so virulent that it went the round of the stables, the loss being 'inconceivable'. No compensation was granted, although local farmers had been compensated for damage to their land. The then Secretary of State for War promised that no cavalry should pass that way again, but the promise was broken. Sam Darling finally took matters into his own hands and put up a notice stating: 'CAVALRY ARE REQUESTED NOT TO LOITER HERE; BY ORDER'. This, as he succinctly put it, had the desired effect.

Sam Darling was soon training Classics winners: in 1903 the Eclipse Stakes was dubbed 'The Race of the Century' – an extravagant claim only three years in – yet the first three past the post, including Beckhampton-trained Ard Patrick, won eight Classics between them, so the claim was justified. Darling purchased two farms in order to ensure his use of the ground for working the horses. One of these, belonging to the Holford family, had become rather run down: the buildings and land were in poor condition. He installed a farm bailiff in the house, which he later re-named 'Galtee More', after his first Derby winner: the horse was named after the Irish mountains whence he came, and the farm bears the name to this day. Meanwhile Galtee More, the horse, who had

Galteemore Farm House

won six more races in 1897 as well as the Derby, was sold to the Russian Government in 1898 for £20,000. This move may have led to the patronage of the stables by Tsar Nicholas II in the early years of the twentieth century.

Sam Darling made a success of farming; he won prizes for his crops and livestock. He was proud to own the 'largest Dutch barn in the country' which has survived and still, as far as we know, holds that distinction. He used a large barn with a pitch-pine floor as a granary; when not in use meetings were held there, so were celebrations such as Harvest Homes. The village celebrated the Coronation there in 1953, an event remembered with pleasure by those that were there.

The second farm bought by Darling was that of the Pinniger's. Here he made his retirement home, having altered the exterior of the house slightly by the addition of bay windows; and gaining for himself the reputation of having built it. He named it 'Willonyx' after another successful horse, winner of many classic races. Among the outhouses was a riding school, which provided good exercise for his horses in inclement weather. He retired there in 1913. Yet another horse, 'Wildfowler' gave his name to four cottages in the village; their name is usually corrupted to 'Wildflower'. Contemporary photographs show all these buildings smothered in ivy: thankfully for the brickwork this has all been removed.

Sam Darling died on 16th.May,1921. He had been a meticulous man, and left instructions that the streets of Beckhampton should be swept and sanded on the day of his funeral and his coffin carried on a farm cart painted in specific colours. He was buried at East Kennett.

The Darling family consolidated the two village institutions which would remain until the present day: the farm and the racing stables. Thanks to the latter, the name of Beckhampton was now 'on the map', with the village itself happy to remain in its shadow.

S AM DARLING has brought us into the twentieth century, and almost within living memory. His son, Fred, had taken over as trainer upon Sam's retirement in 1913. He carried on the stables' tradition of success, exceeding his father's achievements. And like his father, he maintained methods of strict routine and attention to detail – which even included prescribed dress for the stable lads – instigated by his father. Any deviation from the rules meant instant dismissal, yet he inspired affection from his employees, whom he treated with fairness. He was referred to by all as 'The Governor'.

Between 1913 and 1947 he trained nineteen classic winners, including seven Derby winners and three St.Leger winners. He first became leading trainer in 1926. That year 24 of the Beckhampton horses won 48 races between them, worth £63,408 – over £2million in today's money. Some of the prize money went into building wooden cage-boxes costing £1,500 each. He also installed central heating, but this was not a success, causing coughing in the horses. In 1932 he employed Gordon Richards, already a champion, as first jockey, for a retaining fee of £4,000. 1947 saw five Beckhampton horses running in the Derby: the winner was Owen Tudor, enabling Fred Darling to equal John Porter's record of seven Derby winners.

By now the stables enjoyed Royal patronage. In 1942 King George VI and Queen Elizabeth brought their daughters to visit Beckhampton. The King's horse, Big Game, had just won the 2000 Guineas; his other horse, Sun Chariot, won the 1000 Guineas the following day, going on to win the Derby. The King continued to patronise the stables until his death in 1952, when the royal horses were leased to the Duke of Norfolk during court mourning. After an interval of forty years, the Queen once more sent horses to Beckhampton, and visits them annually. Such visits are strictly private, with most of the residents of the village unaware of Her Majesty's presence.

Fred Darling retired in 1947, due to his declining health. With no family member to take over, the stables went to Noel Murless. Fred retained his interest in horses, running the Blacklands Stud near Calne. He died at Willonyx on 9th.June,1953, three days after a horse bred by him had won the Derby. The stables continued to flourish, and indeed Beckhampton is unique in that each of its seven trainers has won at least one Classic, a reputation of which it can be justifiably proud. But no one could hope to equal Fred Darling's achievements; he and his father were perhaps the greatest contributors to the well-being of village life.

With the stables and farms in the hands of the Darlings, there would have been little change in the village during the early years of the century. Although stable lads earned very little, they were probably better off than agricultural workers, having food and lodging provided by the stables. As we have seen during the last century, wages and living conditions of farm labourers were dire. A country village was thought to be far more unhealthy than the town.

In 1908 a George Brown – possibly the grandson of the philanthropic farmer who had allowed his tenants allotments during the Swing riots, built Beckhampton Grange, the stately Edwardian house glimpsed through the trees

Grange Barrow, in front of Grange Barrow House and stables

north of the Bath road. The house may have replaced an earlier dwelling, since the trees surrounding it are much older. The Grange has always been a private residence. When first built it was richly furnished, with silk wall hangings and expensive fittings. In 1926 it was bought by a Mr. Henry Blagrave, a businessman whose family owned much of Reading. He set up a racing stables, converting the existing stables from the farm next door, now Grange Barrow Farm. He bought Beckhampton Stables in 1950, when Noel Murless was the trainer. Murless left in 1952; after which Sir Gordon Richards and Jeremy Tree jointly leased the stables. Mr Blagrave lived on in Beckhampton, enjoying the Grange and his fabulous wealth.

The village's residents still consisted of landowners and workers, although with the arrival of the twentieth century relationships between the two were becoming less formal; the landowners working just as hard as their employees. Soon a new diversion appeared on the scene. The wonder of the age, the cinema, had arrived. As early as 1912 the New Electric Theatre – later the Palace – opened in Devizes. Two years later the Corn Exchange in Marlborough was converted into a cinema. Not to be outdone, Calne's cinema, also the Palace, opened before 1920. No doubt some of the villagers made their way to witness these marvels, and spend some of their hard-earned money. Marlborough's cinema closed down in 1970; the Palace, Calne, was demolished in the 1970s, but the Palace, Devizes, is there still.

Perhaps some of our villagers went to see the King and Queen in 1907. King Edward VII and Queen Alexandra were visiting Bowood House, and returned to London on the 22nd.July of that year. They travelled by train from Calne, riding to the station in an open carriage, with cheering crowds to see them off.

Beckhampton, in common with most rural areas, still lived life mostly in the style of the nineteenth century when the upheaval that would change the country occurred: the outbreak of the First World War in 1914. By now the wool and cloth industries in the west had died out: the number of sheep in Wiltshire dropped by 90% between 1880 and 1950. More and more of the downs were being ploughed up, and wheat and barley were now the staple crops. Thus Beckhampton's reliance upon sheep, which had lasted since pre-historic times, came to an end.

A memorial in Avebury parish church records the names of fifteen men who died in the Great War. Two of them, Harry and Thomas White, were the uncles of Brian White, a present resident of Beckhampton. They lived in Avebury Trusloe at the time. Brian worked on Galtee More Farm for more than fifty years – and still helps out occasionally. Beckhampton was not hit hard by the war, since the stables and particularly the farm continued to provide employment. But, like everywhere else, it was to benefit from the changes. The war years had brought the country out of the nineteenth century world of horses, wagons, oil lamps and labour-intensive farming into the twentieth century. Developments such as motorised transport, electricity, tarmacadam roads, telephones, wireless, piped water and mains drainage took place with astonishing rapidity in cities; rather more slowly in rural areas. The increasing use of farm machinery – in the Calne area imported US tractors were among the first such machines in the country – coupled with the rise of new industries in towns encouraged an urban drift: the village was imperceptibly changing in character.

An aerial photograph of Beckhampton in 1924 clearly shows the established buildings – the stables, Galtee More farm, Willonyx and its associated outbuildings. The Waggon and Horses is there, as are the houses opposite, but there is no sign of buildings along the lane, where one might have expected to see some of the older cottages. The cob and thatch has yielded to the effects of time, leaving the outline of their gardens, and nothing else. It would be forty years before any substantial building in the village took place.

Not too many people owned cars at this time: Brian White remembers climbing Silbury Hill with friends in the 1930s, resolving to go home when the next car came along. Sometimes it could be a very long wait. Yet there was sufficient transport on the A4 to encourage two Marlborough businessmen, Messrs. Herd and Leader, to apply for the erection of a petrol station to the west of Silbury Hill. The Wiltshire Archaeological and Natural History Society objected, voicing their concerns to the Central Council for the Protection of Rural England. The latter upheld their objections, and in spite of the fact that Herd and Leader had spent 'a considerable sum' and had been granted a licence, the scheme was abandoned. But not forgotten, for later aerial photographs show buildings on the site in 1946; there was a garage and filling station there, together with a café, but their dates are not recorded. Joan Hues remembers a Murray Davis and his mother who lived there: he looked after the petrol pumps while his mother served teas and refreshments. The 1967 excavation of Silbury Hill made use of the 'disused café', but the buildings have not survived, and today the site is a car park and viewing area for the hill.

There was another filling-station opposite the Waggon and Horses, on a site which had contained stables until 1939; (it is now a lay-by, with parking for the pub). It was run, from the 1950s onwards, by Ken Vickers, who lived in

Chestnut Cottages, and, sadly, died in November,2000. Ken worked hard – from seven in the morning until eleven at night, seven days a week. He had some help, but there was little time for the gardening that he so loved. When he started at the filling station, petrol was 3/6d a gallon; oil 1/11d a quart. (17½p and 10p respectively in today's money.) Drivers stopping for petrol would expect to have their windscreens cleaned, (no screenwash in those days) and oil and tyre pressures checked. If they felt so inclined they could pop across the road for a pint of the new Wadworth's 6X beer which then cost 1/6d: (7½p). Today's price varies but is well over £2.00. Ken worked at the filling station until the M4 opened in 1971, and traffic virtually ceased on the A4; this, of course, meant the closure of both filling stations. Ken retired to his garden, and produced, year after year, one of the two finest vegetable gardens in the village, the other being Dennis Blake's.

The inter-war years showed the decline and break-up of some of the great estates. This in turn meant that there were fewer tenant farmers. In Wiltshire, fewer than 10% of farms were owner-occupied in 1914, by 1941 this proportion had risen to 37%. Our own farm of Galtee More was bought by the Hues family in 1925, in whose possession it has been ever since.

There was no building in the village between the wars, but improvements were taking place. The road was laid with tarmacadam before 1920. Electricity had arrived, but its use was sporadic and mostly in the form of generators: it would be the 1930s (1932 in all probability according to modern memory) before mains electricity was installed in some houses, although the stables – the end of the line of supply – were still using a generator in the 1950s; the Waggon and Horses had no electricity in 1946. Devizes railway station was never to know the benefits of electricity – and it closed in 1966. Mains water did not appear until 1953 – in Wildfowler Cottages at least – until then pumps were the order of the day. Even today some properties still have water piped in from the farm. Telephones were available, although, it seems, connection was at the mercy of the Misses Hunter who ran the Avebury exchange. The stables (whose number was Avebury 4) and the farm were connected, but many villagers preferred to use the AA box at the crossroads.

Delivery vans still served the village: hardware, fuel, fish, meat, bread, groceries, fruit and vegetables were all provided. There was little need for the weekly visit to market towns, apart from the obvious social benefits. Farm workers and their wives, who were expected to help out with such tasks as hoeing and weeding, worked hard for their meagre wages. But life had its lighter side, as Dennis Blake remembers: he and some schoolboy friends used to meet in an old shepherd's hut for illicit games of cards. They were discovered by the local 'bobby', who failed to retain any physical evidence of this wrongdoing, and so no action was taken. The boys continued with their games, Sergeant Fox no doubt turning a blind eye.

There would have been few cars during the inter-war years, although the bicycle was gaining in popularity. In the early years of the century there were cycle races along what is now the A4; as traffic increased, these races decreased. Today there is virtually no cycle-racing on our roads; although in 1998 the last Milk Race, which was an annually-held road race covering much of the country, passed along the A4.

It is difficult to pin-point the numbering of roads. As early as 1919, the Ministry of Transport introduced a system of three numbered classes of roads, 1,2 and 3, according to their importance. Later this was modified, and letters were brought into use. The country was divided into six zones, (excluding Scotland, which had zones 7,8 and 9) each with its main 'A' road. Thus the Great North Road and the Great Bath Road became the less romantic A1 and A4 respectively. After perusal of some early maps, the writer concludes that this happened in the early 1930s: probably as a result of the Road Traffic Act of 1930. 'A' roads were of course the important routes, 'B' roads subsidiary. 'C' roads still exist, but are rarely labelled as such. The classification of roads can be, and is altered if the use of it changes; this tends to happen near conurbations; the roads around Beckhampton should be safe with the present system.

The residents of the village were all connected to the farm or the stables at this time. Life was hard, but it was going to get harder with the advent of the Second World War in 1939.

B ECKHAMPTON'S INVOLVEMENT in this second 'war to end all wars' was by providing a Home Guard of some twenty-five men, mostly stable lads, but including the two Hues brothers from Galtee More, and Fred Darling, who was the officer. They were trained at Marlborough. There were a couple of Nissen huts and a searchlight just off the track leading south towards the Tan Hill escarpment, which were manned by soldiers. Tanks occasionally strayed across the fields of Galtee More farm, and due compensation was paid for the damage to crops; but most of the war-time activity was outside the village.

These were the years in which, to most of the country, the sight of an aircraft became less of a novelty. But there would have been military aircraft in the skies around Beckhampton since 1912, when the Central Flying School was established at Upavon. The Royal Flying Corps (later R.A.F.) had a base at Yatesbury, which remained as a training base until the 1960s. It was an extensive airfield, now mostly ploughed up, although some of the buildings remain. Today, military aircraft in our skies are mostly army helicopters or Hercules. The latter, based at Lyneham, will not be seen for much longer, as the closure of that particular base has been announced. During the two Gulf Wars the odd American B 52 has been sighted on its way to or from RAF Fairford. As they are usually flying reasonably low their huge size can be appreciated; on the runway their wings curve over to the ground with the weight of their engines, giving them the appearance of a great wounded bird. There is always the possibility that a 'Stealth' bomber will be observed in the future, as they will be based at Fairford, although the whole idea of these monsters is that they should not be seen.

Apart from aerial activity, Beckhampton was not affected by the war: there was no local bombing. The productivity of farming was all-important, and the main occupation. But present-day residents of the village remember, thanks to their houses being shaken, a less well-known contribution to the war effort: the Beckhampton Proof Range, a gunnery research establishment set on All Cannings Down south of West Kennett and near Wansdyke. Its purpose was to determine the effects of firing on shells and fuses. Inert shells were fired up to sixty thousand feet, and recovered so that their examination could take place. The chalk subsoil in the area was particularly suitable for this activity. Vehicles reached the range through West Kennett village, both the guns themselves and the mechanism for digging out and recovering the shells: the latter resembling a large corkscrew mounted on a lorry. The firing range was used from 1942.

After the war the Ministry of Supply wished the research programme to continue for a length of time of not more than ten years. The use of the range would be restricted, as it always had been, to two to three hours a day, not more than three days a week. Warning notices would be posted. At other times there would be public access, and the land could be used for grazing, or ploughed for arable use. The Ministry also sought the right to close off an 'outer danger area' of some 1600 acres from time to time. Not surprisingly, there were local objections to the scheme. A public enquiry was held at Devizes on 24th.March,1949. Major Allinson, former superintendent of the range, stated that the outer danger area had not been closed since 1946. He also said that of two thousand rounds fired yearly only one fell outside the central area, and that only a direct hit would injure cattle. His case was that continued use of the firing range would have little effect on the local population.

The opposition to the plan was led by Wiltshire County Council, Devizes Rural District Council and the Country Landowners Association. Their joint representative, Mr.J.Scott Henderson, K.C., pointed out that Government Departments already owned one seventh of the county, and it was obvious that the possibility of sharing or using another site had not been considered. He went on to discuss the ten year limit, stating that the people of Wiltshire had no faith in government pledges; citing the broken promise to the people of Imber, who had never been allowed to return to their homes. His vehemence, along with that of other interested bodies (archaeologists, naturalists, walkers) won the day, and the Ministry of Supply agreed to look into the possibility of alternative sites for their research. The enquiry was closed – and so was the firing range. There is no indication today of where the range was sited. The land has returned to agricultural use, the firing range, like the cricket pitch, vanishing for ever. Yet modern-day echoes remain. With the army's artillery ranges around twenty miles away at Larkhill, residents frequently hear the thud of explosions; their windows, like the war-time ones, rattling in sympathy.

The post-war years would see great changes throughout the country; villages were no longer farm workers' dwelling places, they were becoming desirable locations for town workers. New housing, of a size and modernity far beyond the average agricultural worker's wages, sprang up. Cars appeared in driveways, and the ability to shop in towns, coupled with the probable absence of the householder, spelt the death-knell of the deliveryman, although certain daily commodities were still provided. The technical developments of two world wars were making people's lives easier, and conversely, more complicated.

Beckhampton was no exception to this rule, although new houses did not appear until the 1950s and 1960s. With the stables continuing to employ men and women, the village did not entirely lose its character, and to this day it supports an amiable mix across the social classes. With horses to attend to, there is usually plenty of coming and going during the day; the village, thankfully, lacks the dead feeling often associated with 'picture postcard' villages whose inhabitants are all busy in local towns.

One obvious change in the village was the gradual decrease of farm workers. When the present farmer's grandfather bought Galtee More in 1925, he employed fifteen full-time men. Today, only two men are employed, with extra help at busy times such as harvest. The farm kept pace with the changes of the century: as new machines were developed, they were brought into use. Before 1920, farm machinery consisted of stationary traction engines. These could be used for threshing, and ploughing, by pulling the metal blades across the fields. Galtee More's first tractor arrived in the 1920s. This was a metal-wheeled affair, and could only be used for ploughing: there were no other attachments at that time. Because the wheels could damage tarmac, the tractor was kept in the fields, quite a change from the modern monsters with their huge rubber wheels.

The farm's main crops were still wheat and barley, as they had been for hundreds of years. The straw from these crops used to be used for thatching; the bundles were known as 'yelms'. Wheat and other crops had much longer straw then, which was much more vulnerable to high winds and bad weather. As plant breeding improved, the straw became shorter and more robust; thatchers had to look elsewhere for their stock-in-trade. The Hues also kept a dairy herd, supplying the village with fresh milk. There are still a few cattle on the farm, but these are reared for beef.

Life in Beckhampton had changed greatly during the first half of the twentieth century. Two world wars had brought about developments in all areas, but there were even more remarkable inventions yet to be revealed. Ever more sophisticated appliances in the home, television, fax machines, the whole world of computers would make their appearance; virtually everyone's life-style would change as the whirlwind of Technology struck the country.

A FTER THE SECOND WORLD WAR the country shook itself and gradually turned its attention to improving the daily lives of its inhabitants. This could not happen overnight, and for the time being food continued to be rationed, and other war-time restrictions imposed. Gradually such delights as bananas and ice cream came upon the scene; sweets and chocolate became more plentiful, although these were the last items to be de-rationed in 1954. Ordinary people got on with their lives, in Beckhampton, as in other rural areas, the most important occupation being the production of crops.

The village began to take on the appearance which it bears today. 'Greenfields' was the first new house to be built in the 1950s; Joan Hues has lived there ever since. She was able to watch as new houses were put up on both sides of the lane, and other dwellings were altered. The village became a residential area, although with many houses still owned by the stables or the farm, and a substantial number of residents working from home, it could be classified as a 'working village'. Deliveries were and are still made: bread, milk, newspapers and fuel are available; all other commodities have to be purchased in local towns. This state of affairs is, of course, common to rural life throughout the country, as families have become more dependent upon the motor car.

The increase in road traffic, both in volume and weight, led to the replacement of the bridge over the Kennet just east of Silbury Hill in 1950. Further improvements were necessary, and by 1960 the A4 had been widened, at the expense of several houses in West Kennett. Beckhampton crossroads, known as such for centuries, (and remembered as the beginning of the long walk home to airmen based at Yatesbury) became Beckhampton roundabout. The planners are to be commended on an attractive traffic island, based, one supposes, on the shape of the many round barrows in the area. The cottage on its north side was demolished. The AA man, who had stood sentinel in his box at the crossroads, and seen many a child safely across the road, gave up his guardianship: twentieth century life as we know it had begun.

In 1967 a major and high-profile excavation of Silbury Hill took place. Sponsored by the B.B.C. it was meant to be televised live as often as possible; but with a three-year project and very few finds, interest waned. The man in charge was Professor R.J.C.Atkinson, a noted archaeologist. He was supported by various university departments which looked into different aspects of the hill: its flora and fauna, modern and ancient; its geology; recording and identifying any finds. Cardiff University's department of mining was to be responsible for digging the main shaft – which was to join up with the 1849 tunnel – and making the whole thing safe. The tunnel had to be big enough to include a small railway and conveyor belt to remove spoil; telephone and electric cables also had to be laid.

The main aim of this huge exercise was to establish the date of the hill and its composition. Professor Atkinson maintained from the start that any major feature at the centre of the hill would be a bonus. One cannot help thinking that his expectations were probably high. Very detailed records were kept, and as the shaft went deeper into the hill, television pictures were relayed to an audience full of anticipation. The pictures were, however, rather dull; especially as most people owned black-and-white television in those days. Presenters were enthusiastic in pointing out layers of chalk or soil, but there was little to excite the average viewer: no 'treasures' of any sort, and above all, no King Sil on his golden horse.

But one must not belittle the excavation which, if it did not hold television audiences spellbound, contributed tremendously to archaeological knowledge. It achieved its aims, and was able to date the hill at c2660BC, that is, nearly 4,500 years old. Professor Atkinson reported that the hill was composed mostly of chalk, in various sizes and fragments, from local sources. Grass turves and some earth from further afield were also used; the whole built up as a stepped cone, whose steps were then infilled to the present smooth shape. The whole structure was built without a break; it has been calculated that it took over three million man-hours: a statistic which maybe is not as exciting as it should be! Atkinson was of the opinion that it was like 'finding oneself inside an enormously complicated layer cake of gigantic size'. He later likened the dark earth containing chalk fragments to 'Toblerone'. John Chandler has described the hill as 'a gargantuan green blancmange'. What is it about the hill which inspires so many analogies with food? The fact that its shape resembles an up-turned mixing bowl of the old-fashioned type, perhaps. Other observers have seen a resemblance to the female form, associated with pregnancy; Silbury becomes the 'earth-mother' figure. All these comparisons indicate the continuing fascination of the hill.

In 1967 there were a few finds of note, but from the top and sides of the hill: a brooch, odd bits of Saxon and Norman fabrics, iron nails, and a silver farthing dated 1010AD (the reign of Ethelred II). These finds seem to have disappeared – they are certainly not in local museums. The excavation ended in 1970. In his summary, Professor Atkinson stated that 'no trace of any structure, deposit or ancient disturbance was found in the small area near the centre which had not previously been explored'. And so the third and by far the most major excavation came to an end having thrown light on the composition and age of the hill, but leaving the reason for its construction still a matter of conjecture.

So it might have remained, but for events in the early twenty-first century. In May, 2000, a hole appeared in the top of the hill. Small holes had appeared previously – and disappeared subsequently. This one was somewhat larger, though, and upon examination it was found that the eighteenth century excavation shaft had collapsed, leaving a hole about six feet wide and of indeterminate depth – forty to fifty feet at least. The hole was fenced off and officially declared unavailable to the public; with a guard during the summer months. This did not deter people from climbing the hill, passing the sometimes sleeping guard on the way. Two intrepid (and highly illegal) souls filmed themselves actually in the shaft, but the local media did not approve, and it is doubtful whether they made any money from their daring, but rather stupid, venture.

Meanwhile months were passing with no further action on the hole in the hill. The National Trust and English Heritage, who were jointly responsible for the care of the hill, were deciding which of them should take on the repair and restoration work. Eventually the burden fell upon English Heritage. The very wet autumn and cold winter which followed took their toll, and the hole became a gaping chasm twenty feet across. This time a high metal fence was erected on top of the hill, (which was removed, to the delight of local residents, in March,2004). A large plastic sheet was put over the hole, but this proved impracticable, as it was very difficult to keep it in place.

English Heritage decided that a thorough investigation of Silbury should be made before the hole was repaired. This could only be done by sound, because of the dense nature of the hill, with sensors placed well inside. The concern was that there may have been side shafts from the main shaft, which could render the hill unstable. In August,2001, a complete seismic study was carried out. Before this could begin, the void in the top of the hill had to be filled with bags of chalk, in order to obtain accurate readings. This was achieved with the use of a small 'Noddy' helicopter, providing a day's entertainment for local inhabitants. The seismic study took several weeks to complete. Scars were left on the hill where equipment had been hauled up, but Nature has healed these since. It was many months before any results were made known.

In February,2002, when the first report was published, perhaps the most important revelation was that the hill is stable. The big surprise was that it had been built in spiral form, not as a series of concentric circular platforms, as had previously been supposed from internal excavations. Also, the hill appears to be polygonal, having nine sides. From above, it would resemble a spider's web. A fragment of an antler pick found on top of the hill confirmed Professor Atkinson's dating. No evidence of a burial was found; there was no central chamber. It is doubtful whether these findings will finally put paid to the legend of King Sil, and why should they?

Every civilisation has its myths and legends which are preserved to enlighten subsequent generations, and a monument such as Silbury Hill is bound to give rise to many stories. There is another common legend about Silbury's origin; that of the Devil carrying a spadeful of earth with which to bury Marlborough/Devizes, (depending on your point of view). He met a cobbler carrying a sack of shoes to be repaired. Upon being asked the distance to the town, the cobbler showed the Devil the worn-out shoes, insisting that they had been used on the walk from whichever town. Hearing this, the Devil dropped the earth by the roadside, and Silbury Hill was born. This legend is also applied to many a hill throughout the country.

It is now thought that the hill was built for purely ceremonial purposes, possibly connected with Avebury. It lies between the two stone avenues, but has no direct link with the circles that can be traced today. We can only speculate as to its use: but a mound of this size – the biggest in Europe – must have been of vital importance in its time. We tend to forget that when newly-built, Silbury would have been white. It takes little imagination to create the impact upon our forbears on first sighting the hill, surrounded by a moat – in winter, if not permanently – with a causewayed approach from the south.

Modern technology has revealed how and when the hill was built, and its original shape. But the huge question of why? remains, and is likely to remain. It is perhaps fitting that Silbury is still an enigma – we need a little mystery in our lives. At the time of writing, English Heritage is appraising the various means of repair to be carried out. To a regular traveller on the A4, the hill is a common sight, though not, one hopes, one to be taken for granted. The fact that it has stood for thousands of years and withstood modern man's intrusions is a testament to the extraordinary skill and expertise of Bronze Age Man.

The road at the foot of Silbury, the A4, was becoming increasingly busy in the 1960s, and less able to cope with the traffic which it was carrying. All over the country that modern phenomenon, the Motorway, was springing up. The M4 was opened in 1971, and overnight Beckhampton became once more a backwater, no doubt to the relief of its residents. The road which had once been a life-saver to the village had become too busy for comfort. Today its busy times are predictable, and avoided if possible.

The stables were still producing Classic winners, and in 1975 Jeremy Tree won the Oaks and the Irish Oaks, thereby making an interesting link with the past. The horse in question, Juliette Marny, was ridden on both occasions by Lester Piggott, great-great-great grandson of John Barnham Day, who had ridden Beckhampton's first Classic winner in 1839. Jeremy Tree invited Roger Charlton to become his assistant in 1977, and the following year Prince Khalid Abdulla sent some of his horses to the stables, leading to many successes. His patronage continues to this day. Tree resigned his trainership in 1989, when Roger Charlton took over. He won the Derby in 1990 with Quest For Fame, the tenth time a Beckhampton horse had won this race.

Roger Charlton, trainer, in Beckhampton House yard

Another of Roger Charlton's horses, Danehill, a handsome bay, became the most successful stallion in the world. As well as his success in this country, he regularly travelled to Australia, where there are at least thirty of his sons at stud, and Ireland. In 2004, two of his offspring won major prizes: Punctilious at Ascot, and North Light in the Derby. Sadly, he died in 2003 as a result of a broken leg. One of his descendants, Kind, is at the stables today. His name is immortalised in Danehill Cottage, home of Jane Brunning, who illustrated this book.

The only other major change in the area at this time was the creation of the World Heritage Site centred on Avebury in 1986. Again, the residents can be grateful, for this means that virtually no building can take place, that verges are kept clean, and that bus shelters are infinitely superior to those around.

By now, snowstorms were not the major hazards that they had been in coaching days, although in 1982 there was deep snow in the Marlborough area. But Beckhampton, although protected to some extent, is fairly high up on the Downs, and subject to high winds and gales. Thus the famous hurricane of 1987 damaged the Hues' Dutch barn. The westerly bay was demolished, leaving the barn with 19 bays. It is still, probably, the longest in the country, and as barns are not built in that style today, it is likely to remain so.

One cannot leave the twentieth century without reference to a modern-day enigma – that of crop circles; a common sight in our fields in the spring and early summer. The originals of these extraordinary features were probably natural: they were very small single circles – some only a few feet across. The sight of them must have triggered the imagination of a few brave – or foolhardy – souls. Over the years, circles of increasing size and complexity have appeared. Nowadays they attract crowds from all over the country – often the world. Some of them are very beautiful; all of them, these days, are meticulously planned. But by whom? Many people believe that they are manifestations of an other-worldly presence, and point, as evidence, to failure of electricity or other unexplained occurrences. Most believe that they are carried out during the hours of darkness, with the use of poles, planks, and quantities of rope. Given the complicated designs, this is quite an achievement, for which the perpetrators must remain anonymous: the coachloads of people, and the helicopters overhead being their public appreciation.

The farmers take a different view. David Hues says that it is not just the current year's damage that is annoying; the following year the damaged crop will re-grow through the present crop, at best irritating, at worst disastrous. Such considerations will not deter the mysterious 'crop circlers' they will continue, no doubt, to provide their controversial puzzles all over the country, but particularly in Wiltshire. An unexpected bonus has occurred recently, as more fields are left fallow, or 'set-aside' in modern-day parlance: if there has been a crop circle in such fields, the outline will be picked out in green the following year – the result can be most attractive – and harmless.

Towards the end of the century, on August 11th,1999, a total eclipse of the sun took place, which was visible in this country. Wiltshire was outside the area of 'totality' i.e. where the sun would disappear completely, which was in the extreme West country. Nevertheless, the 'darkness at noonday' was most impressive. From the Tan Hill escarpment, car headlights and some streetlights could be seen in Pewsey Vale; birds roosted and a few bats made their appearance. Crowds which had gathered, with various musical instruments and much singing, fell silent as the dusk gathered. The sun – a very thin sliver like an early new moon – was visible at times to the naked eye, thanks to clouds which had obscured the whole thing in Cornwall. At the deepest moment of the eclipse, the clouds parted, and the sun was greeted with whoops of joy. A memorable occasion indeed. There will not be another total eclipse in this country until the year 2090: again only visible as total in the West country. Some children who saw this eclipse may see the next – but they will be in their nineties. Most of us will be long dead.

At the end of 1999 the village, in common with most of the country, looked both forwards and backwards. The twentieth century had seen many more changes in the lifestyle of residents than preceding centuries: the demise of sheep-farming; the change in the 'landlord and peasant' regime; the growth of private housing. But thoughts were directed mostly forwards to the new millennium. The village, or settlement, had already witnessed at least three such events: for the present residents, the prospect was a once in a lifetime event, and to be marked as such.

J ANUARY IST. 2000 – a fittingly beautiful day. There was action in Silbury Court, (not the village manor house, alas, but the courtyard development converted from Mr.Pinniger's outbuildings) whose occupants were getting the outdoors party ready. The sun shone: there was little need for the fire in an old oil drum supplied by David Hues. Champagne and mulled wine flowed, and at least half the village welcomed the twenty-first century in style.

Later that year the book written by some of the villagers was launched; again in Silbury Court, again in bright sunshine. The day had begun with a visit to the stables (a visit to the farm had taken place earlier that year in July). Roger Charlton welcomed us and showed us – among other things – the Queen's livery; it was a festive morning and much enjoyed. After lunch the book was distributed to villagers. It is hoped that copies will remain with houses as their occupants leave and are replaced by new owners, so that some record of the village will remain. There was an unexpected bonus in a 'fly-past' by the Red Arrows – they were on their way to Biggin Hill, and will never be aware of the stir they caused in Beckhampton that day! To complete the day we held a Harvest Supper at the Waggon and Horses, splendidly organised by Douglas and Georgina Shepherd.

In December,2000 the western end of the village was flooded for a fortnight: access and egress was via the Devizes road. David Hues put in trenches across the field, but the council had to step in with larger excavators before a ditch deep enough to take away the floodwater was put in. The following spring was wetter than usual: it was April before one could go to the post box without the use of wellies!

June, 2002 marked the Queen's Golden Jubilee, and the village celebrated with an 'all-comers' party. The barn used fifty years previously for the Coronation, although a most attractive building, was deemed too small for the numbers expected, (at the time of writing, it has been let to a bespoke furniture maker.) David Hues allowed us the use of one of his big barns, and after several well-attended and convivial meetings in The Waggon to plan the event, all was ready on the day. A wet day, as it turned out, with showers all morning. Undeterred, the villagers set about decorating the barn with bunting, and collecting and setting out tables and chairs. Nearly 150 people turned up: slightly more than the population of the village. Lunch was taken, then Roger Hues spoke briefly, referring to the Coronation party, at which he had been present, and expressing his pleasure at the success of the present party. The showers relented long enough for children's games and races to take place on the lawn. The day was rounded off with supper in The Waggon and Horses – Douglas and Georgina once more laying on a magnificent spread. The occasion was voted a huge success, with the hope that it, or something similar, might be repeated before the Diamond Jubilee.

And so – what of the future?

Since the year 2000 a number of families with young children have moved into the village, and there is a lively population of under-16s. Present trends indicate that most of them will move away as they grow up, but we must hope that they will look back on their childhood in Beckhampton with pleasure.

The farm and the stables will continue to be important elements in the village. David Hues thinks that farming will become more environmentally aware. Already farmers are leaving margins round the edge of fields in order to

Chester, a local resident

preserve wild life; it is hoped that both flora and fauna will take advantage of these areas. Some hedges are being re-planted. The traceability of crops will be all-important as quality improves. There will always be a demand for food somewhere in the world, especially as weather seems to be getting more extreme. On the vexed question of GM crops, David feels sure that they will be introduced in time, although at present the public needs to be much better informed about the whole issue.

There is an exciting new development on the farm, opposite the Dutch barn. A new state-of-the-art grain dryer and store has been built. This will not be in use until the summer of the year 2005, as the machinery is not yet complete. The barn is huge: fifty metres long by twenty-eight metres wide, and about forty metres high at the apex. St. James' church at Avebury would fit inside comfortably, including the porch and most of the tower. Let us hope that some sort of ceremony will take place when the mighty beast stirs into action.

Windmill Hill neolithic site, the Bronze Age cemetery to the right, with the Galteemore Farm Dutch barn and new grain store in the foreground

The stables will continue to thrive, and produce winners, although with the huge competition these days in the world of horse-racing, it may not equal the Darling's success. Its employees will still live in the village; the clip-clop of horses' hooves along the lane will not cease; the village will continue to co-exist in the past and in the present. It will maintain its twentieth-century role of a pleasant residential area.

In the wider context, hares will still chase about on the downs, the skylarks will sing above them. The stones at Avebury and the surrounding barrows will stand as a permanent reminder of ages past; the stealth bombers a reminder of ages to come.

Beckhampton has survived and will survive, and will always remain, in the view of those who know it, a special place whose essence time will not alter.

Appendix 1
Owners of the Manor of Beckhampton

1190 Hilary of Beckhampton
1235 & 1242-3   Hamon of Beckhampton
1268 John, son of Richard of Beckhampton
1302 Moieties split:

Joan, wife of Sir Henry le
Moyne, d.1340
Descended with the manor of
Shipton Moyne to John
(grandson) d.1381
1428 Sir John Moyne
John Stourton
1462 William, Lord Stourton
(d..1478)
1467 son, John, (d.1485)

brothers William and Edward,
both d.1524
 son, William, sold moiety to
William Button, d.1549
Remained in Button family
until Ambrose sold the estate
to
1596 Richard Trusloe
1614 John
1638 Portion of estate sold to

1316 Richard Casterton
1428 Geoffrey Casterton
Remained in Casterton family
until
1445 Richard Casterton
succeeded by daughter
Elizabeth
1503 & 1547 probably held by John
Colville (d.1552)
1561 moiety sold by William Saville
and his wife, Anne
1573 John Mitchell sold it to
Thomas Goddard of Upham
Remained in the Goddard
family until sold to Charles
Tooker [see column 1, next
page]

Thomas Smith [see column 2, this page] remainder to John's son

1692 John

1702 sold to Charles Tooker, who acquired the other moiety

1710 Both moieties sold to Sir Richard Holford
Grandson Richard

1731 Uncle Robert
Sons Robert & Peter (d.1803)
Sons: Robert (d.1838)
George (d.1839)
Grandson Robert Staynor Holford (d.1892)
Great-grandson George Lindsay Holford

1897 Sold to Sam Darling (d.1921)

1638 portion sold to Thomas Smith: passed with West Kennet Manor to great-grandson Thomas Smith

1713 sold to Daniel Dyke
probably before 1743 acquired by John Beake

1749 sold to Prince Sutton (d.1779) son James

1801 daughters: Eleanor, wife of T.Estcourt
Sarah, wife of J.Matthews

1804 Sarah and James conveyed their rights to Estcourt

1815 Farm held by Anthony Guy

1828 bought by Thomas Pinniger
Remained in the Pinniger family until 1900 bought by Sam Darling.

Estate broken up – son Fred retained 670 acres.

1947 sold to J.A.Dewar

1950 sold to Mr.H.G.Blagrave

1969 Beckhampton Estates.

Appendix 2
Highlights in the history of
Beckhampton Stables

1745 Beckhampton House is built.

1835 Arrival of **BILLY TREEN.**

1839 Fulwar Craven's *Deception* (J.B.Day) wins The Oaks
Mr.W.Treen's *Barnacles* (P.Conolly) wins the Goodwood Stakes.

1850 Captain Henry Archdall's *Windisgratz* (G.Mann) wins the Goodwood Stakes.

1855 Closure of the Inn.

1862 Mr.James Smith's *Hartington* (J.Grimshaw) wins the Cesarewitch.

1867 Arrival of **HARRY WOOLCOTT.**

1868 Mr.William Graham's *Formosa* (G.Fordham) runs a dead heat in the 2,000 Guineas and wins the 1,000 Guineas and Oaks. *Formosa* (T.Chaloner) wins the St.Leger.

1870 Mr.William Graham's *Gamos* (G.Fordham) wins the Oaks.
Mr.J.G.Hessey's *Sabinus* (Rowell) wins the City and Suburban, Great Metropolitan Handicaps, and the Gold Cup.

1877 Sir George Chetwynd's *Chypre* (C.Wood) wins the Ascot Stakes.

1882 **SAM DARLING** buys Beckhampton House.

1894 Mr.John Gubbins' *Blairfinde* (T.Garrett) wins the Irish Derby.

1895 Mr.John Gubbins' *Galtee More* (M.Cannon) wins the Middle Park Plate.

1897 *Galtee More* (C.Wood) wins the 2,000 Guineas, Derby and St.Leger.

1898 Captain Henry Greer's *Wildfowler* (C.Wood) wins the St.Leger.

1901 Mr.Foxall Keene's *Cap and Bells 11* (M.Henry) wins the Oaks.

1902 Mr.John Gubbins' *Ard Patrick* (J.H.Martin) wins the Derby.

1903 *Ard Patrick* (O.Madden) wins the Eclipse Stakes. (Dubbed the Race of the Century.)

1907 Captain Henry Greer's *Slieve Gallion* (W.Higgs) wins the 2,000 Guineas.

1911 Mr.Charles Howard's *Willonyx* (W.Higgs) wins the Chester Cup, Ascot Stakes, Gold Cup, Cesarewitch, and Jockey Club Cup.

1913 **SAM DARLING** retires, his son, **FRED DARLING** takes over.

1916 Mr.James Buchanan's *Hurry On* (C.Childs) wins the St.Leger.

1922 Lord Woolavington's (formerly Mr.James Buchanan) *Captain Cuttle* (S.Donoghue) wins the Derby.

1925 Mr.H.E.Morriss's *Manna* (S.Donoghue) wins the 2,000 Guineas and Derby,

1926 Lord Woolavington's *Coronach* (J.Childs) wins the Derby and St.Leger. Beckhampton is champion stable.

1931 Mr.J.A.Dewar's *Cameronian* (J.Childs) wins the 2,000 Guineas. Earl of Ellesmere's *Four Course* (E.C.Elliott) wins the 1,000 Guineas. *Cameronian* (F.Fox) wins the Derby.

1932 Gordon Richards becomes Beckhampton stable jockey.

1933 Earl of Lonsdale's *Myrobella* (G.Richards) wins the July Cup. Lord Woolavington's *Maureen* (G.Richards) wins the Queen Mary Stakes. Mr.J.A.Dewar's *Medieval Knight* (G.Richards) wins the Coventry Stakes and Middle Park Stakes. Mr.H.E.Morriss's *Tai-Yang* (G.Richards) wins the Jockey Club Stakes. Beckhampton is champion stable.

1935 Mr.J.A.Dewar's *Fair Trial* (G.Richards) wins the Queen Anne Stakes.

1938 Mr.H.E.Morriss's *Pasch* (G.Richards) wins the 2,000 Guineas and Eclipse Stakes. Mr.Peter Beatty's *Bois Roussel* (E.C.Elliott) wins the Derby.

1940 Mr.F.Darling's *Pont L'Eveque* (S.Wragg) wins the Derby. Beckhampton is champion stable.

1941 Mrs.Reginald Macdonald-Buchanan's *Owen Tudor* (W.Nevett) wins the Derby. Mr.J.A.Dewar's *Commotion* (H.Wragg) wins the Oaks. H.M.King George VI's *Sun Chariot* (H.Wragg) wins the Middle Park Stakes. The King's *Big Game* (H.Wragg) wins the Coventry Stakes.

Beckhampton is champion stable.

1942 *Sun Chariot* (G.Richards) wins the 1,000 Guineas, Oaks and St.Leger.

Big Game (G.Richards) wins the 2,000 Guineas.

Owen Tudor (G.Richards) wins the Gold Cup.

Beckhampton is champion stable.

1947 Mr.J.A.Tudor's *Tudor Minstrel* (G.Richards) wins the 2,000 Guineas.

The King's *Blue Train* (G.Richards) wins the Newmarket Stakes.

Beckhampton is champion stable.

FRED DARLING retires due to ill health.

Beckhampton House Stable is sold to Mr.J.A.Dewar, **NOEL MURLESS** is trainer.

1948 Sir Percy Loraine's *Queenpot* (G.Richards) wins the 1,000 Guineas.

Mr.F.Darling's *Goblet* (G.Richards) wins the Nassau Stakes.

Major Reginald Macdonald-Buchanan's *Abernant* (C.Smirke) wins the Chesham Stakes.

Abernant (G.Richards) wins the Champagne Stakes and Middle Park Stakes.

Major Macdonald-Buchanan's *Royal Forest* (G.Richards) wins the Coventry Stakes.

Royal Forest (G.Richards) wins the Dewhurst Stakes.

Beckhampton is champion stable.

1949 Mr.G.R.H.Smith's *Ridge Wood* (M.Beary) wins the St.Leger.

Abernant (G.Richards) wins the King's Stand Stakes, The July Cup, the King George Stakes and the Nunthorpe Stakes.

Royal Forest (G.Richards) wins the Gordon Stakes.

Earl of Feversham's *Krakatao* (G.Richards) wins the Sussex Stakes.

1950 *Abernant* (G.Richards) wins the July Cup, King George Stakes and Nunthorpe Stakes.

Lt-Col. Giles Loder's *Abadan* (G.Richards) wins the Diadem Stakes.

1951 Lt-Col. Giles Loder's *Sea Parrot* (G.Richards) wins the Nassau Stakes and the Yorkshire Oaks.

1952 Beckhampton House Stable is sold to Mr. H.G.Blagrave. **JEREMY TREE** is trainer.

1955 Mr.J.Tree's *Double Bore* (T.Gosling) wins the Goodwood Cup.

1960 Mr.J.H.Whitney's *Persian Road* (G.Moore) wins the Ebor Handicap.

1963 Miss Monica Sheriffe's *Only For Life* (J.Lindley) wins the 2,000 Guineas and King Edward VII Stakes.

Major J.G.Morrison's *Spree* (J.Lindley) wins the Nassau Stakes.

1964 Mr.Charles Englehard's *Double Jump* (J.Lindley) is champion two-year-old, winning the National Breeders' Produce Stakes and Gimcrack Stakes.

1968 Mr.J.H.Whitney's *D'Urberville* (J.Mercer) wins the King's Stand Stakes.
Miss Monica Sheriffe's *The Elk* (W.Pyers) wins the Observer Gold Cup.

1971 Mr.J.H.Whitney's *Swing Easy* (L.Piggott) wins the King's Stand Stakes and Nunthorpe Stakes.

1975 Mr.James Morrison's *Juliette Marny* (L.Piggott) wins the Oaks and Irish Oaks.

1976 Mr.J.H.Whitney's *John Cherry* (L.Piggott) wins the Chester Cup and the Cesarewitch.

1979 Mr.Khalid Abdulla's *Abeer* (W.Carson) wins the Queen Mary Stakes.
Mr.James Morrison's *Scintillate* (Pat Eddery) wins the Oaks.
Mr.Khalid Abdulla's *Known Fact* (W.Carson) wins the Middle Park Stakes.

1980 *Known Fact* (W.Carson) wins the 2,000 Guineas, Waterford Crystal Mile and Queen Elizabeth II Stakes.
Miss Monica Sheriffe's *Sharpo* (Pat Eddery) wins the William Hill Sprint Championship.
Sharpo (Pat Eddery) wins the Prix de Saint-Georges and William Hill Sprint Championship.

1982 *Sharpo* (Pat Eddery) wins the July Cup and Prix de L'Abbaye de Longchamp.
Sharpo (S.Cauthen) wins the William Hill Sprint Championship.
Mr.J.H.Whitney, who had bought the stable from Mr.H.G.Blagrave, dies. His bequest to British racing was the establishment of Beckhampton as a training stable in perpetuity, as far as was legally practical, for which a trust fund was set up under the terms of his will.

1984 Mr.Khalid Abdulla's *Rainbow Quest* (Pat Eddery) wins the Great Voltigeur Stakes.

1985 *Rainbow Quest* (Pat Eddery) wins the Prix de L'Arc de Triomphe and Coronation Cup.
Mr.Khalid Abdulla's *Damister* (S.Cauthen) wins the Guardian Classic Trial.
Damister (Pat Eddery) wins the Mecca-Dante Stakes and Great Voltigeur Stakes.
Mr.Khalid Abdulla's *Kingscote* (Pat Eddery) wins the Lowther Stakes.

1986 Mr.R.J.McCreery's *Orange Hill* (R.Fox) wins the Cesarewitch.
Mr.Stavros Niarchos's *Valuable Witness* (Pat Eddery) wins the Jockey Club Cup.

1989 *Two Timing* (Pat Eddery) wins the Prince of Wales' Stakes;
True Panache (Pat Eddery) wins the Royal Hunt Cup and
Danehill (W.Carson) wins the Cork and Orrery Stakes for Mr.Khalid Abdulla at Royal Ascot.
JEREMY TREE retires, **ROGER CHARLTON** becomes trainer.

1990 Mr.Khalid Abdulla's *Sanglamore* (Pat Eddery) wins the French Derby.
Mr. Khalid Abdulla's *Quest For Fame* (Pat Eddery) wins the English Derby.

1991 *Sanglamore* (Pat Eddery) wins the Prix d'Isaphan.

1993 Mr A Oppenheimer's *Inchinor* (L.Dettori) wins the Greenham Stakes

1996 Lady Rothschild's *Spout* (Tim Sprake) wins The Lancashire Oaks
Mr M Myer's *Cap Juluca* (Richard Hughes) wins the Cambridgeshire

1997 Mr K Abdulla's *Wixim* (Pat Eddery) wins the Sandown Mile

1998 Highclere Thoroughbreds' *Tamarisk* (Tim Sprake) wins the Haydock Sprint.

1999 Mrs A Chandris's *Harmonic Way* (Richard Hughes) wins The Stewards Cup
Mrs A Chandris's *Harmonic Way* (Richard Hughes) wins The Cork and Orrery Stakes

2000 Mrs A Chandris's *Harmonic Way* (Richard Hughes) wins The Wokingham

2002 Team Valor's *Luvah Girl* (Kevin Darley) wins the The Owen Brown Rockfel Stakes

2003 Mr K Abdulla's *Three Valleys* (USA) (Richard Hughes) wins the Coventry Stakes
Mr. D.J. Deer's *Patevellian* (Steve Drowne) wins the Prix de l'Abbaye
Mr D J Deer's *Patavellian* (Ire) (S.Drowne) wins The Vodafone Stewards Cup
Mr D J Deer's *Patavellian* (Ire) (S.Drowne) wins The Bunbury Cup

2004 Mr B Nielsen's *Tante Rose* (Ire) (Richard Hughes) wins the Haydock Sprint

Bibliography

Wiltshire Archaeological and Natural History Magazine.
Victoria History of Wiltshire, Volumes III, IV, XII.

BETTEY, J.H. *Wessex from AD 1000*, Longman, 1986.
BETTEY, J.H. *Rural Life in Wessex, 1500 – 1900*, Alan Sutton, 1987.
BURL, Aubrey. *Prehistoric Avebury*. Yale University Press, 1979.
CHANDLER, John. *A Sense of Belonging*. Ex Libris Press, 1998.
CHANDLER, John. *Marlborough and Eastern Wiltshire*. Hobnob Press, 2001.
CHANDLER, John, *Devizes and Central Wiltshire*. Hobnob Press, 2003.
DARLING, Sam. *Sam Darling's Reminiscences*. Mills & Boon, 1914.
ELLIS, Peter. *Roman Wiltshire and After*. W.A.N.H..S. 2001.
FARMER, David, Ed. *Oxford Dictionary of Saints*. O.U.P. 5th. Edition, 2003.
HAYCOCK, Lorna. *Devizes, History and Guide*. Alan Sutton, 2000.
HOARE, Sir Richard Colt. *The Ancient History of North Wiltshire*. London, 1821.
MARSH, A.E.W. *A History of the Borough and Town of Calne*. Castle, Lamb &
    Storr, 1903.
POLLARD, Joshua, REYNOLDS, Andrew, *Avebury: The Biography of a
    Landscape*. Tempus, 2002.
PHILLIPS, Daphne, *The Great Road to Bath*. Countryside Books, 1983.
STUKELEY, William, *Abury, A Temple of the British Druids*. London, 1743.
TAYLOR,C.C. *Village and Farmstead*. George Philip, 1983.
UNDERDOWN, David. *Revel, Riot and Rebellion*. O.U.P. 1985.
WATTS, Kenneth. *The Marlborough Downs*. Ex Libris Press, 1993.
WHITTLE, Alasdair. *Sacred Mound, Holy Rings*. Oxbow Monograph 74. 1997.

I am also indebted to:

Wiltshire & Swindon Record Office, Trowbridge.

Wiltshire County Council, Archaeology Department, Trowbridge.

The combined universities archaeological team, led by:

      Joshua Pollard, now University of Bristol.

      Mark Gillings, University of Leicester.

      David Wheatley, University of Southampton.

Staff at Marlborough and Devizes Public Libraries.

Index

This is a selective index of persons and places only. It omits the two appendices (pages 77-83) and the names of racehorses. Places in Beckhampton are separately indexed.